AWAKENED IDENTITY

AWAKENED IDENTITY

Unlock the Power of Sonship and Ekklesia to Change the World

GREG SIMAS

Foreword by BILL JOHNSON

Copyright © 2025 by Greg Simas

All rights reserved. No part of this book may be used or reproduced in any manner whatsoever without prior written consent of the author, except as provided by the United States of America copyright law.

Published by Best Seller Publishing®, St. Augustine, FL
Best Seller Publishing® is a registered trademark.
Printed in the United States of America.

ISBN: 978-1969338724

This publication is designed to provide accurate and authoritative information with regard to the subject matter covered. It is sold with the understanding that the publisher is not engaged in rendering legal, accounting, or other professional advice. If legal advice or other expert assistance is required, the services of a competent professional should be sought. The opinions expressed by the author in this book are not endorsed by Best Seller Publishing® and are the sole responsibility of the author rendering the opinion.

For more information, please write:
Best Seller Publishing®
1775 US-1 #1070
St. Augustine, FL 32084
or call 1 (626) 765-9750
Visit us online at: www.BestSellerPublishing.org

Dedication

To the Father—who called me His son and awakened my identity.

To Wendi, my wife and lifelong friend in this journey.

To my family—Andrew and Hannah, Jordan, Billy, and Lydia—and to all my incredible grandchildren. Your love, encouragement, and unwavering support have always inspired me to pursue the calling God has placed on my life.

To my Convergence Church family, who have walked this path with me and embraced an awakened identity.

This book is as much yours as it is mine.

Acknowledgments

I'm grateful for those who, over the years, have prophesied over me and encouraged me to write. Your willingness to step out has helped bring this book into reality. I'm also thankful for the team at Best Selling Publishers for partnering with me in the creation and release of *Awakened Identity*. Above all, I thank the Lord for His grace, His revelation, and the privilege of writing this book in partnership with Him.

Scripture Acknowledgments

Unless otherwise noted, all Scripture quotations are taken from the **New King James Version®**. Copyright © 1982 by Thomas Nelson. Used by permission. All rights reserved.

Scripture quotations marked **TPT** are taken from **The Passion Translation®**. Copyright © 2017, 2018 by Passion & Fire Ministries, Inc. Used by permission. All rights reserved. The Passion Translation® and The Passion Translation® logo are registered trademarks of Passion & Fire Ministries, Inc.

Scripture quotations marked **NLT** are taken from the **Holy Bible, New Living Translation**, copyright © 1996, 2004, 2015 by Tyndale House Foundation. Used by permission of **Tyndale House Publishers, Inc., Carol Stream, Illinois 60188**. All rights reserved.

Scripture quotations marked **NIV** are taken from the **Holy Bible, New International Version®, NIV®**. Copyright © 1973, 1978, 1984, 2011 by **Biblica, Inc.™** Used by permission. All rights reserved worldwide. "NIV" and "New International Version" are trademarks registered in the United States Patent and Trademark Office by Biblica, Inc.™

All rights to these translations are fully retained by their respective copyright holders.

Contents

Dedication v
Acknowledgments vii
Scripture Acknowledgments ix

Foreword 1
Preface 3

Section One: Sonship 5
  1. The Revelation of the Father 7
  2. From Orphan to Sonship 19
  3. Religion vs. Relationship 31
  4. Living From Sonship 39

Section Two: Ekklesia 51
  5. From Sonship to Ekklesia 53
  6. The Original Operating System 69
  7. Restoring the Church as the Ekklesia 83

Section Three: Change the World 97
  8. The Convergence of Sonship and Ekklesia 99
  9. Beyond the Walls 113
 10. The World Awaits 127
 11. This is Your Time 141

About the Author 153

Foreword

We were designed for a seamless connection with God: spirit, soul, and body. He made us in His image for the purpose of relationship. And His ultimate dream is that from this place of unhindered connection, we would co-labor with Him to see His world shape the realities of this one. This is the privilege of each believer. And as my friend Lou Engle says, "God had a dream, and He wrapped you around it."

All co-laboring with God must come from a place of confident assurance, knowing who He is and who we are as sons and daughters of the King. Even Jesus's own initiation into ministry was propelled by the Father's declaration: "This is my son in whom I'm well pleased" (Matthew 3:17).

This book is a treasure, written by my brother-in-law and friend, Greg Simas. Greg draws from the wisdom obtained from over forty years of ministry experience, and gifts us with this priceless tool, *Awakened Identity: Unlock the Power of Sonship and Ekklesia to Change the World*. His passion for equipping the Body of Christ is evident on each page. Over the years, I've been able to witness his journey of living out the convergence of both identity (sonship) and purpose (Ekklesia). This book is the result and is a wonderful resource to help establish the God-given identity, purpose, and destiny of each reader. You will receive insight and be encouraged and inspired.

I often tell our pastoral staff that I'm not interested in building a big church. My goal is to build big people—those who walk confidently in their identity as sons and daughters, standing on the two legs of *purity* and *power*, committed to representing Him well. Our primary call is not to maintain buildings or build organizations, as helpful as they are. Nor are we here to perform religious routines without eternal purpose. We are called as ambassadors, co-laboring with God to see the kingdom of heaven be made manifest here, until the whole earth is "filled with the knowledge of the glory of God" (Habakkuk 2:14).

How we live is dictated by how we think. It's why we are instructed in Romans 12:2 to "be transformed by the renewing of your mind." We are only as transformed as our mind is renewed. This book is a wonderful gift, introducing us to the mind of Christ: how Jesus thinks about us. I am excited to see the impact of this book and how it will equip the saints for eternal purpose. Please read it, and pass it on to others!

Bill Johnson
Senior Leader, Bethel Church, Redding
Author of *Born for Significance* and *The Holy Spirit*

Preface

Thank you for picking up *Awakened Identity*. This book is the fruit of years spent preaching, teaching, and walking with countless individuals—both within our local church community and across nations. Again and again, I've encountered believers who genuinely love God, yet still live disconnected from the identity and purpose they were created for. That consistent theme is what led me to write this book—not to offer a theory, but to invite you into the fullness of your identity—an identity that both awakens purpose and redefines your life.

At its core, this book unpacks three foundational realities that lead to lasting transformation: Sonship, Ekklesia, and our calling to change the world. Sonship anchors us in our true identity as sons and daughters of the Father. Ekklesia empowers us to function as Heaven's representatives on Earth. And together, they awaken us to live lives that carry the power and presence of God into every sphere of society. My prayer is that as you read, something awakens in you—not just information, but revelation. May these truths not only challenge you but deeply change you, just as they've changed me.

SECTION ONE

Sonship

Sonship
Father

1.
The Revelation of the Father

Years ago, I was officiating a wedding for a couple getting married in my church. As the wedding rehearsal unfolded, a moment meant to symbolize love and unity took an unexpected turn, revealing a deeper truth about the nature of parental affection. The soon-to-be bride, Vivian, a 39-year-old Asian woman, stood with her father at the crucial "giving away" part of the ceremony. This tradition, where a father embraces his daughter and then welcomes the groom, is a powerful act of love and acceptance.

However, when I asked Vivian's father to hug his daughter, an awkward silence filled the room. His hesitation was noticeable. Sensing something was off, Vivian quietly confessed, "My father has never hugged me." I was stunned by her words. How could a father go through life without ever embracing his daughter, showing her physical affection, and tangibly releasing the love and security she desperately needed?

Determined to create this moment for them, I encouraged him again. Awkwardly, he put his arms around her. The instant his embrace encircled her, Vivian broke down in tears. In that single embrace walls came down and a father's love broke through. Like Vivian, we all need to know the embrace of our Father and the experience of His love.

How I Found the Father

Growing up in a Catholic household, I attended catechism classes regularly, where I was introduced to various aspects of the Catholic faith through flannel board presentations and other teaching tools. While Jesus was relatable, God the Father was a remote and somewhat vague figure who oversaw and directed all things behind the scenes but was not directly involved in the affairs of humanity. This perception couldn't be made any clearer than as depicted in Michelangelo's painting on the ceiling of the Sistine Chapel. In that image, the Father reaches out to touch Adam but never makes contact. This is how I saw the Father: just out of my reach.

At the age of 16, my life took a significant turn. I experienced the profound, life-changing moment of salvation when I gave my life entirely to Jesus. This personal encounter with Christ was transformative, igniting a deep passion and commitment to follow Him. Jesus changed my life so dramatically and completely that others who knew me before my salvation could not believe the change.

My understanding of God was now centered around Jesus, the author and finisher of my faith. Jesus was both relatable and approachable. He wasn't distant or removed; He was present, tangible, and compassionate.

This newfound relationship with Jesus was life-changing. For the first time, I felt a personal connection with God, filling an eternal void in my heart. I was saved and set free.

My prayers and worship were directed toward Christ, and while I acknowledged the Father, I didn't truly know Him. Jesus became the focal point of my faith, and though this was profoundly enriching, it left an unexplored dimension of my relationship with God untouched.

At 19, another transformative experience occurred when I was baptized in the Holy Spirit. This event ignited a passion within me, launching me into full-time ministry. The Holy Spirit brought a dynamic, empowering presence into my life, leading me to deeper biblical insights, the boldness to share my faith, and spiritual gifts, including signs, wonders, and miracles. Yet, despite these profound experiences with Jesus and the Holy Spirit, my relationship with the Father remained distant. The truth is, I never really considered a relationship with the Father, because it was never something I was taught to pursue. I thought then that Jesus and the Holy Spirit were enough.

So, once again, the Father was a background figure in my relationship with God. I had no idea how much the Father wanted to have a relationship with me. I didn't realize it then, but my relationship with God was like a three-legged stool with only two legs, missing the revelation of the Father that both reveals and anchors my identity.

Bible College and Pulpits

Back then, when God called you to full-time ministry, generally the next step was to attend Bible college. Since I was born again in an Assemblies of God church, I went to a spirit-filled Assemblies of God Bible college—Bethany Bible College. With my sights set on a lifetime of ministry, I chose to pursue and graduate with an accredited ministerial degree.

While there, I was immersed in theology as I was being trained for the ministry. Courses on Christology, Pneumatology, and Ecclesiology were part of the core theology curriculum, each offering rich insights into different dimensions of the Christian faith. However, just like in church, no classes, courses, or weekend seminars on studying or exploring God as Father existed!

This gap was not just a personal observation from one Bible college but a widespread issue across all Bible colleges and seminaries. In my research, I could not find one Bible college or seminary with a core theological class on God the Father. If there are any, they're few and far between. I graduated from Bible college knowing more about the devil and demons than I knew about the Father.

In addition, as I think back, I don't remember hearing a message or series of messages on God as Father. Zero. And I've been around a while! I can safely say that the messaging on God as Father is not on pastors' preaching calendars year in and year out. Like a drought that plagues the land, we are experiencing a drought, albeit a severe one, on teaching and preaching about God as Father. Unlike Jesus, who constantly pointed to the Father, the church and Bible colleges have remained almost entirely silent.

The Central Issue

I firmly believe that knowing and encountering the heart of the Father is the central issue profoundly missing in the church today. That's a big statement, but I make it with unwavering conviction. Born out of four decades of personal experience as a believer and pastor, I've seen that many in the church (including myself for many years) are living as spiritual orphans instead of sons and daughters. And the tragedy is, most don't even know it. The good news is that the tide is turning. For years, I've witnessed firsthand the transformative power of knowing God as Father and encountering His Father's heart.

This revelation is not merely another theological concept to be added to our intellectual understanding, though its theological importance cannot be overstated. It is an ongoing, life-changing encounter that goes beyond knowledge and doctrine. When individuals truly experience the heart of the Father, it brings about a dramatic transformation that glorifies Him in every aspect of their lives.

I've seen this evidence in countless lives changed, hearts healed, and relationships restored. This profound encounter with the Father moves us from a place of mere religious duty to a vibrant, intimate relationship with Him. It shifts our identity from servants to sons and daughters, fully embraced and loved by our Heavenly Father.

Let me ask you a few questions. What was the ultimate reason for Jesus's coming? What was His mission? What was the ultimate purpose of the cross and resurrection? These are thought-provoking questions. I'm sure we can all say the reason for Jesus's coming was to demonstrate the love of God, to provide a way for us to be saved, redeemed, and reconciled to God, to destroy the power of sin and the works of the devil, in our lives and the world. But "unto what" exactly? Why did He do this? What's the ultimate reason, the end goal? We find the answer in John 14:6.

> **John 14:6** I am the way, the truth and the life, no one comes to the Father except through me."

I propose that the ultimate purpose of Jesus's coming—the "unto what" of His mission—was to bring us to the Father! While receiving Jesus into our hearts secures our salvation, it also grants us something even more remarkable: access to the Father. I've read and quoted John 14:6 thousands of times, yet somehow missed this connection.

In addition, Jesus's purpose was not only to provide a *path* to the Father but also to show humanity *who* the Father is. He made a powerful statement when He said, "If you have seen me, you've seen the Father" (John 14:9). Jesus was so closely connected to the Father that simply seeing and hearing Him revealed the nature of the Father.

Not only that, but His mission included demonstrating who the Father is by how He lived. Listen in as Jesus prays to His Father regarding the disciples in John 17, just before His betrayal and arrest in Gethsemane.

> **John 17:26** (TPT): "I have **revealed** to them who you are, and I will **continue** to make you even more real to them, so that they may **experience** the same endless love that you have for me, for your love will now live in them, even as I live in them!

Jesus revealed the Father and is still revealing Him today, inviting us into a continual experience in the Father's love.

Jesus's relationship with the Father was so vital that He did nothing independently; He only did what he *saw* His Father doing.

> **John 5:19** (NLT) So Jesus explained, "I tell you the truth, the Son can do nothing by himself. *He does only what he sees the Father doing.* Whatever the Father does, the Son also does."

Jesus lived each day in response to what He saw His Father doing, with the sole purpose of revealing who the Father is. In fact, if you have seen Jesus, you have seen the Father. The ultimate goal of His life and mission, including the cross, is to bring us to the Father and into Sonship. So why is there almost complete silence on who the Father is when Jesus gave everything to reveal Him and to bring us to Him?

I must admit, it puzzled me. But more accurately, it frustrated me. Why didn't anyone tell me about the Father's love? My view of the Father was distant. I lived much of my Christian life from the foundation of duty. Orphaned. Disconnected. Whatever I did, I felt it wasn't quite enough. I needed to do more. Be more. Read the Bible more. Pray more. Share my faith more. Have you ever felt like this?

My lack of knowledge regarding the heart and embrace of the Father left me lacking in the full revelation of my Sonship. As much as I love the supernatural, revival, the Presence, seeing souls saved, reaching cities for Christ, and a host of other things, I largely missed the very purpose of Christ coming and my own salvation, that is, to bring me into an ongoing encounter with the love of the Father. So I found myself living like the elder brother in the story of the prodigal son. Though I was a son, I had the mindset of a slave. I didn't realize the full extent of this until I encountered the love of the Father for myself.

Fatherless World

Our nation is wrestling with a multitude of deeply troubling issues. A brief scroll through social media or a few minutes of TV time reveals the moral decline and division that is upon us. Some would argue that the most severe problems we face in America are crime, corruption, racism, gender identity, pornography, sex trafficking, and abortion. Countless books and articles have been written about these serious concerns. The severe gravity of these issues should concern us all and must be addressed.

But what we don't see much in the news and social media is the effect fatherlessness has as the foundation to all that is stated above. Though we don't have time in this volume to delve deeper into this, I can say to you that the absence of the father in a child's life has created far-reaching negative consequences and significant problems in the home and, in a broader sense, our neighborhoods, cities, and country. This is not just in homes where a father is not living, but this also applies to homes where the father lives but is absent and disconnected from their child's life.

On one occasion, as a guest speaker at a local church, I preached on receiving the Father's embrace and then offered a father's embrace to anyone in need—a prophetic act demonstrating the heart and love of their Heavenly Father. A 61-year-old man and his wife approached me, and he shared with me that his father was cruel and abusive. His father would chase him with a chainsaw and tell him to throw himself into the wood-burning fireplace. His father would also say that if he ever told his mother, the father would kill her. Though he was saved early in life and faithfully followed Jesus, his perception of his Heavenly Father was clouded by the way his earthly father treated him. And since our pulpits are virtually silent about who our Heavenly Father is, he lived his life up to this point with the understanding that he was never enough and could never do enough to win his Heavenly Father's love and approval. He lived spiritually orphaned. That all changed when I put my arms around him and asked him to receive the Father's embrace. As he hugged me, something in him broke. He left a changed man, a better husband and father.

A mother and daughter came to me, both in tears. The mother, 56 years old, was divorced, and her daughter, in her 20s, never knew her biological father. The mother shared that she had never received an embrace from her father, and the daughter, deeply emotional, had also never experienced a father's embrace. They were followers of Jesus, baptized with the Holy Spirit, but had not encountered the love of the Heavenly Father. My heart went out to both as I put my arms around each of them, declaring that my arms were His arms and to receive the embrace of their Heavenly Father.

Recently, in our School of Ministry, a 66-year-old man testified that his earthly father left him when he was only 5 years old. He found the Lord in his teenage years and faithfully served Him in his home and church. When he testified, he said, "For 61 years, I did not know who my Heavenly Father was until now!" Sixty-one years is too long to miss who Jesus came to reveal: that is, the Father.

These people sit in our churches, attend regularly, and serve faithfully.

Personally, I was determined to remain faithful to the end, giving my life sacrificially to the cause of Christ. I was committed to doing whatever He told me to do and going wherever He told me to go. However, because I didn't understand the depth of the Father's love for me, I constantly felt He was not fully pleased with me and sensed His disappointment whenever I wasn't doing "more." I realized I was living my Christian life as an orphan rather than a son, seeking to earn God's love and affection instead of living from it.

Revelation of the Father

Jesus's connection to the Father was so vital that He didn't start His ministry until He received the love and affirmation of being a beloved Son. His identity with the Father came first, paving the way for His ministry for the Father. We see this clearly at His baptism in Matthew 3:17.

Matthew 3:17 And suddenly a voice came from Heaven, saying, "This is My beloved Son, in whom I am well pleased."

This connection with the Father was the launching pad for everything Jesus did on Earth. Before this event, Jesus hadn't performed any miracles, preached any sermons, or called any disciples. He had no public platform, no social media following, and no podcasts. What He had was something far more important: the revelation of the Father's love and His identity as a beloved Son. This was the foundation that sustained Him in both life and ministry.

When we study Jesus's life, we often focus on His teachings, miracles, and incredible demonstrations of the Kingdom of God. These are essential, yet little time is devoted to studying His relationship with the Father and His mission to make the Father known to His disciples and the world.

The revelation of the Father's heart and knowing our identity as sons and daughters is so essential that Satan directly challenges Jesus on this very issue—His identity as a Son. Right after His baptism, Jesus is led into the wilderness to be tempted by the devil for forty days. The devil's temptations specifically target Jesus's identity:

Matthew 4:3 Now when the tempter came to Him, he said, *"If You are the Son of God,* command that these stones become bread."

Matthew 4:5-6 Then the devil took Him up into the holy city, set Him on the pinnacle of the temple, and said to Him, *"If You are the Son of God,* throw Yourself down. For it is written: He shall give His angels charge over you,' In their hands, they shall bear you up, Lest you dash your foot against a stone.'

Jesus did not need to prove His Sonship. His Father made it clear at His baptism. There was no need to perform. Jesus was already fully loved and accepted. The temptation had no foothold in Jesus's life because His identity was already established.

Jesus fulfilled His earthly ministry in *response* to His Sonship, not to prove it. He lived life and did ministry *from* approval, not for it. The battle over identity *preceded* His fruitfulness in ministry.

Jesus is our example. Our life and ministry should flow out of an encounter with the Father's love and the revelation that we are His beloved sons and daughters. But if the church remains silent on who the Father is, and if we as believers lack understanding of His heart, we risk living as spiritual orphans rather than as sons and daughters, often without even realizing it. This lack of revelation unknowingly crucifies the resurrected life and disconnects us from our Father.

In the chapter that follows, we will delve more into this orphan state and why we must move past it.

2.
From Orphan to Sonship

For decades, I've preached from the Bible with sincere motives, integrity, and a profound sense of awe. It's a privilege beyond measure to steward His Word and communicate His heart to His people. In carrying out this responsibility, I've always sought to preach the full counsel of God's Word to the congregation I lead. And while I have done my best to do that over the years, I now see that the revelation of the Father and our adoption into Sonship is one of the most foundational truths we can teach. Yet, for much of my ministry I rarely taught on this, not because I ignored the subject but simply because I had not yet received the full revelation regarding it.

Without the revelation of the Father active in my life, I realized that I was pastoring, preaching, and teaching from an orphaned heart. I prayed, read the Word, and did all that was expected of me as both a disciple and pastor. I viewed myself primarily as a servant, living and ministering for the Lord. But beneath the surface, I felt constant pressure to be better, do more, and prove my devotion through what I achieved.

I would go so far as to say that many pastors and leaders are in the same place, carrying an *orphan heart* without even realizing it. I believe that trying to *prove* their love for God by working hard and striving for visible results is one of the main contributors to the widespread burnout and moral failures seen in church and ministry leadership. I'm not against hard work or measurable results in ministry, I believe in both, but they must flow *from* the love of God, not as an attempt to *prove* it. Without the revelation and encounter of the Father's love, the weight of ministry is just too much to bear. It's that important!

If our pulpits are orphaned, our congregations will be too. If pastors and leaders have little revelation or encounter with the Father's love, they will unintentionally convey this lack to those they serve and lead. How could they not? We can't live and teach what we don't know.

What, then, is an orphan heart, and how do we identify it? More importantly, what is it in contrast to? This is where we start. We need a revelation of what Jesus paid for and what He has brought us into when we become born again.

The Orphan Heart

The concept of the "orphan heart" is a profound and deeply rooted issue that affects our relationship with God and others. We will define the "orphan heart" as a mindset or emotional state characterized by a deep sense of disconnection and abandonment from the Father's love and care, creating feelings of rejection, isolation, and lack of belonging, even if one is not an orphan. This mindset manifests as insecurity and a relentless pursuit of approval, rooted in the belief that one is not truly accepted or valued by the Father. Essentially, it is a mindset of struggling to feel fully loved and accepted for who one truly is in Christ.

In John 14:15-18, Jesus reassures His disciples that He will not leave them as orphans but will come to them. This promise extends beyond the disciples to all of humanity, addressing a fundamental human condition. The orphan heart feels abandoned, fatherless, and disconnected from the source of true love and identity—God the Father.

The origin of the orphan heart can be traced back to Lucifer's rebellion against God, as described in Isaiah 14 and Ezekiel 28. Lucifer chose to live independently from God, rejecting His fatherhood, and thus became spiritually orphaned. His "corrupted wisdom" aims to bring humanity into this state of "orphan-ness," like himself, encouraging a life independent of the Father. This same orphaned state was passed down to humanity when Adam and Eve sinned and were banished from the Garden of Eden. As a result, they lost their intimate fellowship with God, causing humanity to become spiritually orphaned.

James Jordan, a Christian author and speaker, explains that humanity's fundamental problem is its orphaned state:

> When this perspective dawned on me I felt, for the first time in my life, that I began to understand the basic problem of humanity. The basic problem is not only of our individual struggles, but also the struggles that we have in relationship with each other. The basic problem of church life, the friction between denominations, family disputes and even the wars between nations. I suddenly saw the root problem of humanity's struggle on this earth throughout history. It was a complete paradigm shift. Someone said to me once, "James, you seem to think that the Father's love is the answer to every problem in humanity." I believe that with all of my heart, because every problem has its foundation in the fact that Adam and Eve lost their place in Eden, lost their place in the Father experientially loving them! When

that happened, the human race fell from God's total provision and lost intimate fellowship with Him.[1] [NOTE: USED WITH AUTHOR'S PERMISSION]

This orphaned heart—born from a lack of revelation and experience of the Father's love—affects every aspect of life, from our personal struggles and relationships to church culture, and even global conflicts. The root of all these issues is losing our place in the Father's love and provision. When Adam and Eve fell, they lost their experiential knowledge of God's love, and humanity has been striving to fill that void ever since.

The orphan heart manifests in various ways and includes feelings of rejection, insecurity, and a constant need for approval. This state of the heart is not merely a psychological issue but a spiritual one that requires a deep, transformative encounter with the Father's love through Jesus Christ.

An orphan heart is marked by striving, competition, and a constant search for approval and significance, living as if there is no secure and loving place in the Father's embrace. It carries a deep sense of disconnection, lacking the affirmation, protection, comfort, and belonging that come from knowing Him as a true Father. This often leads to feelings of loneliness and isolation, driving one to try to earn love, success, or significance through achievement and performance. Without a rooted sense of Sonship, even those who know Christ can find themselves constantly battling anxiety, fear, and frustration, never fully resting in the inheritance freely given by God.

A person with an orphan heart often feels they must earn everything they get in life. They may be saved, but they live as if they are not fully accepted and loved by God. This mindset

---

[1] Jordan, M. James. *Sonship: The Journey into the Father's Heart.* Fatherheart Ministries, 2007. Chapter 4.

can lead to self-medication through addictions, workaholism, or other forms of escapism.

The story of the prodigal son illustrates the difference between an orphan heart and a heart of Sonship. The elder son had his father's affection and the full inheritance of a son, yet he lived with the mindset of a slave—believing he had to earn his father's approval and resenting his brother's restoration. In contrast, despite his mistakes, the younger son experienced the Father's unconditional love and acceptance upon his return.

A sense of emptiness and spiritual fatigue also marks the orphan heart. There is an ongoing feeling of not being entirely accepted and lovingly cared for by the Father. This leads to a critical and cynical outlook on life. Worship becomes problematic because it requires drawing near to God, and it's hard to draw near if you feel you're not accepted. Receiving love from others is also challenging because an orphan heart struggles to believe they can be fully loved. This leads to a lack of trust and a tendency to test the authenticity of others' love.

For some, the orphan-hearted person turns to self-medication to ease the pain. This can be found in addictions to work, overeating, abusing alcohol, sex outside the boundaries of marriage, pornography, misuse of pain medications—anything to medicate the pain they are in. The Father of all Comfort (2 Corinthians 1:3,4) cannot be approached because the orphan-hearted person is convinced that the Father is distant and feel that they are not worth pursuing or being loved.

Spiritual Adoption

The orphan-hearted way of living is not the inheritance of the believer. We've been adopted, but until that truth becomes revelation, we remain stuck in an identity that isn't ours.

Ephesians 1:3-6 explains that we have been blessed with every spiritual blessing and chosen for adoption as sons through Jesus Christ. This passage reveals the depth of God's love and plan for us, predestined before the foundation of the world, to come into Sonship through the sacrificial death of Jesus. In other words, through adoption, we are positioned to encounter the love and embrace of the Father.

Galatians 3:26-4:7 elaborates on this adoption, stating that through faith in Christ, we become sons of God and heirs according to the promise. This adoption is more than a legal status; it is a transformative process that moves us from bondage to freedom, from slavery to Sonship. Scripture emphasizes that in Christ, there is no distinction between Jew or Greek, slave or free, male or female—we are all one in Him and, thus, heirs of God's promises.

When we think of adoption, we often picture a child who, living outside a family, is legally brought into another family through a formal process. This child gains new parents, a new home, and a renewed sense of belonging and identity. When we see the word "adoption" in the Bible, we immediately have this view in mind. The biblical view of adoption is different than our current view. Let me explain.

The ancient Roman ceremony of "son placing" offers significant insight into adoption. In the New Testament context, adoption comes from the word huiothesia, the Greek term meaning "son placing." In Galatians 4:1-7, Apostle Paul uses this cultural practice to illustrate Roman adoption and our spiritual transition through Christ. In this Roman context, before the ceremony, a child was under the care of guardians and stewards and had no more rights than a slave. At the appointed time, usually the early teenage years, a public ceremony was held at the gates of the city where the father formally *placed* (adopted) the child as a son, giving him full legal rights as a son and heir, making the transition from servanthood to Sonship.

Paul's metaphor of spiritual adoption through this ceremony highlights a profound transformation. Just as Roman sons were granted full rights and responsibilities, spiritual adoption confers Sonship on every believer. When we receive Christ, we are instantly *placed* as sons and daughters based on His finished work. We don't earn our Sonship; it's given to us as a gift by grace through faith. Because of Christ's completed work on the cross as the Son of God, those of us who are in Him have been placed as sons and daughters with full approval and access to the Father!

The implications are monumental; this adoption moves us from a position of subservience and insecurity to one of authority and privilege in God's household.

From Slave to Son

The transformation from being bound by sin to being restored as sons and daughters by the Father lies at the heart of the Gospel. Galatians 4:3-7 explains that once, humanity was in bondage under the elements of the world. Sin had made us slaves, separated from God, and bound by worldly chains. But "when the fullness of the time had come, God sent forth His Son, born of a woman, born under the law, to redeem those who were under the law, that we might receive the adoption as sons."

Through Jesus's redemptive work, we are no longer slaves but sons. This transition signifies a complete renewal of identity and relationship with God as Father, restoring us to our rightful place as His children with all associated rights and privileges.

We are empowered, cherished, and secure in our Father's love. Romans 8:15–17 reinforces this truth:

> For you did not receive the spirit of bondage again to fear, but you received the Spirit of adoption by whom we cry out, *"Abba, Father."* The Spirit Himself bears witness with our spirit that we are children of God, and if children, then heirs—heirs of God and joint heirs with Christ, if indeed we suffer with Him, that we may also be glorified together.

This passage highlights the word "Abba," which is Aramaic for the most affectionate word a child can name their father, meaning daddy. One of the most significant hurdles I have overcome is reconciling God's holiness with Abba Father. I have always felt that God is too holy to be called Daddy. But the scriptures bear this out. As much as He is Holy, He is also *Abba*. Galatians 4:6 says, "And because you are sons, God has sent forth the Spirit of His Son into your hearts, crying out, 'Abba, Father!'" This revelation of Abba Father is so essential that one of the primary roles of the Holy Spirit is to convince us of its reality. The Spirit inside us cries out, "Abba, Father—Daddy God."

The term "Abba" signifies an intimate relationship with God the Father, similar to the relationship Jesus had. The intimacy we share with God through the Spirit, who cries "Abba, Father," allows us to experience a closeness and relationship with the Father that quite frankly is unimaginable but nonetheless real. This new intimacy is not based on fear or obligation but on love and trust, reflecting our secure position in God's family. It grants us full rights as sons and daughters, moving us from bondage to freedom, from orphans to heirs. Our significance now derives from our position in Christ as sons and daughters rather than duty and performance, enabling us to fulfill God's purpose for our lives. This is what the cross provides. This is the gospel. And it's all a gift.

This knowledge of being adopted by grace shapes our sense of value and identity in Christ, leading us to minister *from* love, not *for* it. When we embrace our identity as sons and daughters, we are empowered to live confidently and purposefully, knowing that our value is rooted in the love of the Father and not our self-efforts.

Our new standing before God is one of freedom and honor. As sons and daughters, we are given full access to the Father's love, guidance, and inheritance. This privileged position empowers us to live out our faith with confidence and joy, knowing that our Heavenly Father deeply loves and values us.

Embracing Sonship

The transition from an orphan heart to a heart of Sonship begins with understanding and accepting our identity as God's children. Romans 8:14–24 speaks of the "Spirit of full acceptance" that enfolds us into the family of God. The Holy Spirit longs to make God's fatherhood real to us, whispering into our innermost being that we are His children.

As the Holy Spirit brings us the revelation of the Fathers love, we grow in our Sonship, and to experience the Father's love and approval in deeper ways. We understand that we are heirs of God and co-heirs with Christ. This means we share in His glory and inheritance. Our lives are no longer driven by a need to earn God's love but rest in it.

Living as sons and daughters of God transforms our perspective and behavior. We see God as our loving Father rather than a distant master. We live *from* His love rather than working *for* it. We focus on our God-given destiny rather than our troubled past. We live by the law of love rather than the love of the law. We experience God's presence and comfort rather than seeking counterfeit affection.

A heart of Sonship is characterized by humility and compassion. We value others and rejoice in their successes. We see correction as a blessing and an opportunity for growth. We are open, patient, and affectionate, laying down our lives to meet the needs of others. We live in freedom and liberty, experiencing the Father's unconditional love and acceptance.

The transformation from an orphan heart to a heart of Sonship requires the continual renewal of our minds. It requires us to let go of the lies and misconceptions we have believed about ourselves and God, and replace them with the truth of God's Word and promises. The Holy Spirit facilitates this process, continually reminding us of our identity and worth in Christ.

Practical Steps Forward

How do we begin to live from this place of Sonship? It starts with cultivating a growing revelation of the Father's love. We must intentionally position ourselves to receive His love, believing that the transformation we need will flow from His heart into ours. This means coming before Him honestly, with all our baggage, pain, and shortcomings. It means trusting that He delights in us, even in our weakness. As we do this consistently, His love begins to heal our orphan mindsets and rewire how we relate to Him and others.

Jesus's teaching in John 15 about abiding in the vine beautifully illustrates this. Our role is to remain connected to

Him, receiving His life-giving love and allowing it to bear fruit through us.

As we learn to abide in the Father's love and let it shape our identity, we begin to see the stark contrast between living from Sonship and striving under religion. True Sonship is rooted in receiving, not earning—yet many of us have unknowingly carried a mindset shaped by religion rather than relationship. Before we can fully embrace this life-giving reality, we must recognize and dismantle the religious structures that keep us from experiencing the Father's love. In the next chapter, we will explore this contrast, uncovering the difference between striving for approval and living from the security of Sonship.

3.
Religion vs. Relationship

In its many forms, religion is often humanity's attempt to reach up to God through rituals, works, and sacrifices, hoping to gain His favor or avoid His displeasure. It is a system created by humanity that places the burden of connection and approval squarely on our shoulders. We strive, we struggle, and we hope that, somehow, our efforts will be enough.

However, the gospel of Christ turns this notion on its head. The gospel flows down from the heart of God. It originates in the Father's love, not in our attempts to reach Him. God is not a distant deity waiting to be appeased; He is a loving Father who initiated reconciliation through the life, death, and resurrection of Jesus Christ. Our relationship with Him is not based on our ability to perform or meet religious standards but on His unchanging love and grace.

As A.W. Tozer, pastor and author, profoundly stated, *"What comes into our minds when we think about God is the most important thing about us."*[2] If we see God as a harsh taskmaster, our lives will reflect that perception—marked by fear, striving, and uncertainty. But if we see Him as our loving Father, we

---

[2] Tozer, A.W. *The Knowledge of the Holy*. Harper & Row, 1961.

will live from a place of security, peace, and rest. This is the difference between religion and relationship. Religion seeks to earn and maintain God's approval; relationship rest in it.

Orphan Efforts

I've always had a heart for revival, and that passion still burns within me. I long to see the glory of the Lord fill the Earth—to witness His light breaking through, transforming lives in a way that nothing else can. Still, I lived under a belief system that told me if I did all the right things—if I worked hard enough, pursued the anointing, attended revival conferences, and traveled to the "wells of revival"—then revival would surely come. While these things are not wrong in and of themselves, I sincerely believed that if I worked hard enough and did all the right things, God would respond with revival the way I envisioned.

Looking back, I see now that this mindset stemmed from a religious framework and an orphaned heart. I believed that if I checked all the right boxes and avoided making mistakes, if I sought out the right people who carried "the anointing," then revival will happen. But when it didn't unfold as I expected, I was left questioning myself, wondering what I was doing wrong. Why wasn't God moving the way I thought He would? Why did He seem to be blessing others more than me? Deep down, I felt overlooked and passed by, and I questioned whether I was as loved or favored by the Lord as others appeared to be.

This is a dangerous place where even good desires—like the desire for revival—can become distorted by wrong mindsets. I daresay it's a product of religious mindsets and orphaned thinking. When revival becomes something we think we can earn by checking all the right boxes, we can fall into the trap of religious performance. We unintentionally turn revival into a goal to be achieved rather than a move that flows from the heart of God.

I don't have time to recount the many stories of pastors, leaders, marriages, and families that have been shipwrecked through this pursuit. Striving can lead to burnout, which comes from operating within a religious and orphaned mindset, even when the pursuit is revival itself. For many, the relentless striving for revival—believing it depends on our work and effort—has led others into discouragement and disillusionment. Some have given up entirely, losing their ministries, families, and even their faith along the way, chasing after a move of God but missing the heart of God.

Revival is relational at its core. It's not tied to the size of our churches or how many conferences we attend. It's about the Father's love being made manifest to the world by the Holy Spirit. When our hearts are filled with His love—when we live in the fullness of our identity as His sons and daughters—revival has a foundation to flow freely, not because we've worked for it, but because His presence cannot help but transform everything it touches.

When we are not fully convinced of God's love and goodness, we can easily fall prey to the trap of religious systems. These systems are born out of a disconnection with God as Father, resulting in the need to earn His favor through our self-efforts. We may find ourselves working tirelessly to maintain our right standing with God, driven by a fear of losing His favor and love. This upward striving creates an unending cycle that leads to burnout, condemnation, and a loss of joy.

In this cycle, we hide our weaknesses and flaws from the Lord, fearing that He would reject us if He truly saw us as we are. But in hiding, we miss the opportunity to experience His transformative love. Our Father desires to meet us in our brokenness and bring healing and restoration. When we are not assured of His love, we generate our own religious efforts to stay on His good side. Over time, this leads to a works-based faith that is more about self-reliance than dependence on God.

The Apostle Paul understood this struggle well. Before his encounter with Christ, he was deeply entrenched in a religious system, boasting in his ability to keep the law and his zeal for God. Yet, after encountering the risen Christ, Paul recognized the futility of his efforts and declared, "Whatever were gains to me I now consider loss for the sake of Christ" (Philippians 3:7 NIV). He realized that true righteousness and connection with God come not from our efforts but by grace through faith in Christ.

As we navigate the Christian life, one of the most significant transformations we can experience is moving from a religious mindset to living out of the fullness of our relationship with the Father as His sons and daughters. This shift changes everything—it awakens our identity, purpose, and the way we interact with the world around us. The difference between religion and relationship is not just a theological nuance; it is the foundation of a vibrant and authentic Christian life.

Transforming Power

Sonship means allowing the Father's love to reshape us from within, transforming how we see ourselves and relate to Him. The Christian life is not a series of tasks to complete or standards to meet; it is a relationship to be embraced. Jesus came to reveal the Father and to draw us into this relationship of unconditional love and acceptance.

Romans 5:5 (TPT) tells us, "we can now experience the endless love of God cascading into our hearts through the Holy

Spirit who lives in us." This love is not something we earn; it is a gift we receive through faith. The transformation we long for comes from this continuous flow of the Father's love. It is the life of God flowing from Heaven to Earth, changing us, and enabling us to live in a way that reflects His character and heart.

When we live from Sonship, we see everything as a gift from the Father. We no longer strive to earn His favor but surrender to the assurance that we are fully loved and accepted. This changes how we approach life, ministry, and our relationship with God. Instead of trying to live *for* God, we learn to live *from* God—allowing His life and love to flow through us and impact the world around us.

The Inner Work of the Holy Spirit

Our Sonship is awakened by the Holy Spirit, who bears witness with our spirit that we are children of God (Romans 8:16). This witness is not merely a feeling but a profound inner assurance that comes from the Spirit's work within us. The Holy Spirit is constantly at work in our hearts, shaping our desires, aligning our will with the Father's, and cultivating the character of Christ in us.

Living from this inner work is essential because the Spirit empowers us to live as sons and daughters. Without His work, our efforts to live out our identity would be nothing more than striving in our own strength, leading to frustration and a constant cycle of feeling that we are not doing enough. But when we rely on the Holy Spirit, He empowers us from within, enabling us to live in a way that reflects our true identity in Christ.

A Transformed Heart

The Christian life is not about behavior modification but heart transformation. The Holy Spirit works deep within us, renewing our minds and transforming our hearts so that our actions naturally align with God's will. This transformation is not something we can accomplish on our own. It is a supernatural work of the Spirit that begins in the innermost parts of our being and manifests outwardly in our daily lives.

Galatians 5:16-17 speaks to this inner conflict between the flesh and the Spirit. Our flesh, or self-life, craves what is contrary to the Spirit. However, as the Holy Spirit works within us, He empowers us to overcome these fleshly desires. This is not a battle we can win through willpower or self-determination. Only through the Spirit's work in us can we walk in victory, living in a way that pleases God.

The Evidence of the Spirit's Work

As the Holy Spirit works within us, the evidence of His presence emerges. We cannot fabricate this evidence; it is the natural outgrowth of the Spirit's power and work in our lives. When the Spirit is at work, our character is transformed, and we begin to exhibit qualities consistent with Christ.

These qualities—often referred to as the fruit of the Spirit—are not produced by human effort but by the Spirit's work within us. They are the markers of a life being transformed from the inside out. When the Holy Spirit is at work in our hearts, love flows naturally, joy is unspeakable, peace prevails, and patience endures. Our interactions with others are marked by kindness, our actions are rooted in goodness, and our faithfulness is unwavering. Gentleness tempers our strength, and self-control governs our passions.

This transformation is not instantaneous; it unfolds over time as we continue to yield to the Holy Spirit's work. The Spirit patiently cultivates these qualities in us, refining us and making us more like Christ. This inner work of the Spirit empowers us to live out our Sonship in a way that glorifies God.

Living from the Inside Out

Living from the Holy Spirit's inner work means living authentically, with our actions flowing from the deep work that the Spirit of God is doing in our hearts. It means that our outward behavior is not a façade but a genuine expression of who we are becoming in Christ. This kind of living requires a continuous openness to the Spirit's work, allowing Him to shape and mold us from the inside out.

We are not driven by external pressures or expectations when we live from the Spirit's transforming work within us. Instead, we are motivated by the Spirit's leading and empowered by His strength. This is the essence of what it means to walk in the Spirit. It is a walk dictated not by the flesh or the law but by the Spirit's work within us.

Living from the inner work of the Holy Spirit also means that we are continually being renewed. The Spirit's work is not a one-time event but an ongoing process. He continually renews our minds and transforms our character. As we live from this place of renewal, we find that our desires align more and more with God's desires, and that our lives increasingly reflect His will.

The Supernatural Life

The journey from religion to relationship is not just a change in mindset, it's a complete transformation on how we live. No longer striving to earn acceptance, we now live as sons and daughters, empowered by the Spirit to walk supernaturally. Living out our Sonship through the inner work of the Holy Spirit is a supernatural way of life. It is a life that goes beyond the natural, beyond what we could achieve on our own. The Spirit's work in us enables us to live in a way that truly reflects our identity as sons and daughters. This is not just about doing good or avoiding sin; it is about being transformed into the likeness of Christ from the inside out.

This supernatural life is marked by the Spirit's power at work within us. It is a life of freedom, where we are no longer enslaved to the desires of the flesh but are empowered to live in the fullness of our Sonship. It is a life of purpose, where every action is infused with meaning because it flows from the Spirit's work in us. And it is a life of impact, where the evidence of the Spirit's work in us becomes a testimony to others of God's transformative power.

When we live from the inside out, we are no longer driven by external pressures or societal expectations. Instead, we are motivated and empowered by the Spirit's leading. This is the essence of walking in the Spirit—not being dictated by the flesh but allowing the Spirit to shape every part of our lives. Living from this place of inner transformation requires continuous openness to the Spirit's work, allowing Him to reshape our minds, hearts, and desires to align with God's purposes... As this transformation becomes evident, it testifies to the world that we are sons and daughters of God, filled with His power and the reality of His love.

4.
Living from Sonship

Growing in Sonship is a lifelong process of transformation, shaping how we think, live, and respond daily. It's not merely a concept to grasp but an invitation to experience the Father's love in a way that changes us from within. Sonship speaks to the core of our identity, freeing us from the need to define ourselves by roles, achievements, or past experiences. Instead, we are shaped by the truth that we are loved, chosen, and pursued by a perfect Father who desires a deep relationship with us. As I fully embraced my identity as a son, I began to see tangible inward Kingdom realities and outward Kingdom responses in my life—evidence of the Father's love and the Spirit's transforming work—reshaping how I saw myself and how I interacted with the world.

Trust the Father

One of the most powerful aspects of this transformation is that it doesn't depend on my ability to measure up or reach a certain level of spiritual maturity. Instead, it's all about my willingness to surrender to the Father's love and trust in His work within me. So often, this growth happens so subtly that I don't even recognize it in the moment. But as I look over the past few years, I can see how much He's been changing me, leading me into greater freedom, and revealing deeper layers of His love at work in my life.

I'm not walking this path of Sonship alone. As I've already stated, the Holy Spirit constantly reminds me of the Father's nearness, teaching me to let go of fear, insecurity, and the limitations I've placed on myself. This process isn't rushed—it's a lifelong invitation to know the Father more deeply and align my life with His heart. I've learned that moments of discomfort or uncertainty aren't signs of the Fathers distance; they're markers of transformation. Every step I take draws me deeper into His embrace, further aligning me with His love and preparing me to walk fully in the identity He created me to live from.

A Vision of What's Possible

As we explore these Kingdom realities and responses, we begin to see a vision of what's truly possible in our lives—lives fully established in Sonship. Each of these realities and responses aren't just goals to pursue; they're invitations to experience the Father's work in our lives firsthand. His transformation is deeply personal and shapes every part of our daily lives.

These aren't just distant theological concepts; they are the very qualities the Father wants to cultivate in us. Each one reflects His nature and reveals the life He has purposed for us to walk in. They are the evidence of what becomes possible when we surrender to His love and yield to the Spirit's leading. Like leaven in dough, the transformation may not always feel dramatic, but it is steady and unstoppable. Every act of surrender, every step of faith, draws us deeper into our true identity, shaping us into the son or daughter He designed us to be.

Sonship isn't just something we believe—it's something we become. Like the metamorphosis of a caterpillar into a butterfly, this transformation is the fulfillment of who we were always meant to be. As we yield to the Father's love and walk in step with the Spirit, these Kingdom realities and responses take root in our lives, aligning us with His design and equipping us for our unique calling.

This is where transformation moves from an internal reality to an outward expression—where Sonship doesn't just change how we see ourselves but completely reshapes how we live. It influences how we think, how we act, and how we interact with the world around us. As we embrace these realities and responses, they become the markers of a life fully lived in the Father's love, revealing what's possible when we walk in our awakened identity.

Inward Realities

Living from Sonship isn't just a theological concept—it transforms daily life. This reality shapes our thoughts, decisions, and interactions, grounding us in the Father's love and positioning us to walk with confidence, purpose, and authority. The more we embrace Sonship, the more we see its impact in the rhythms of our daily lives, from navigating challenges to engaging with others and stewarding what God has given us.

Security is at the core of this transformation—the unshakable assurance that we are chosen, known, and loved by the Father. This changes how we approach life. No longer driven by fear, striving, or the need for approval, we live from a place of rest and confidence. Instead of being tossed by circumstances, we are anchored in the truth of who we are. This means that in daily life, whether at work, in relationships, or when facing uncertainty, we don't react out of insecurity but respond with wisdom and trust. The pressure to prove ourselves fades and is replaced by the joy of simply being His.

This security brings true comfort, not as a momentary escape but as a constant presence that strengthens us. When difficulties arise, we don't need to numb our pain with temporary fixes or seek relief in things that don't last. Instead, we turn to the Father, knowing His comfort is real and unchanging. When we live from Sonship, we bring our struggles to Him first. This daily habit of coming to the Father with our burdens shifts our perspective. Hardships don't have the final say—His love does. Over time, this dependence on Him builds resilience, helping us face life's ups and downs with steady confidence.

This leads us into peace—an active reality that influences every area of our lives. Sonship doesn't promise the absence of storms, but it does promise His presence in the midst of them. Jesus modeled this when He slept in the boat during the storm, completely at peace in the Father's love. That same peace is available to us. When deadlines pile up, unexpected challenges come, or relationships feel strained, we don't have to be ruled by anxiety. Instead, we can lean into His peace, allowing it to govern our emotions and decisions. This peace shifts the way we interact with others. Instead of reacting out of fear or frustration, we become people who bring calm, hope, and clarity into every situation.

This daily reality of peace also impacts how we carry ourselves. A person walking in peace stands out in a world of stress and fear. Whether in conversations, leadership, or family dynamics, those who live from Sonship create peaceful environments where people feel safe, secure, and encouraged. This isn't about feeling good internally—it's a supernatural peace we carry daily. People notice when someone is steady in the face of chaos, and it opens doors for influence and transformation.

From this foundation of security and peace, we step into the authority that Sonship grants us. Walking in authority isn't just about big, dramatic moments—it's about the confidence to live each day knowing we have been given the authority to overcome obstacles. Authority affects the way we pray, speak, and act. It means we don't shrink back in the face of difficulties, but we stand firm, knowing we have access to Heaven's resources. When problems arise, we don't passively accept them—we bring them before the Father and partner with Him in faith to overcome them.

Authority influences our words. When we speak, we do so with the understanding that our words carry Kingdom influence. Whether we encourage a friend, pray over a situation, or make decisions, we do so from a place of assurance, not doubt. This changes how we approach challenges in our homes, workplaces, and communities. We stop seeing obstacles as barriers and start seeing them as opportunities to display God's power.

Living in Sonship also transforms how we view our unique calling. No longer striving to figure out our worth or direction, we step into each day knowing we are positioned exactly where God wants us to be. Whether we are leading a team, raising a family, serving in ministry, or running a business, we do it with the awareness that we are led by the Spirit and are ambassadors of the Kingdom. This shifts how we approach work—no task is insignificant when done in partnership with God. Conversations become opportunities, daily responsibilities become assignments from Heaven, and every interaction carries the potential for impact.

Sonship redefines how we handle provision. Instead of fearing lack, we trust that our Father supplies all our needs. This trust frees us from comparison and striving. When we stop worrying about having enough, we become generous, living open-handedly and stewarding what God has given us. We recognize that provision isn't just about finances—it's about wisdom in making decisions, and favor in our assignments.

As we grow in Sonship, our daily lives begin to reflect the realities of the Kingdom. We move with confidence, trusting that God is leading us. We live with peace and refuse to be shaken by circumstances. We walk in authority, knowing we have been sent to bring transformation. We live with purpose, seeing every moment as an opportunity to advance the Kingdom. This is the daily impact of Sonship—everything changes as we step into our true identity.

When we live from Sonship, we don't just experience these realities internally; they overflow into the lives of those around us. Our families, workplaces, and communities are transformed because we live as sons and daughters who know who they are. This is the power of an awakened identity. As we embrace it, we don't just change personally—we become agents of change, carrying the presence and purpose of the Father everywhere we go.

Outward Responses

When the supernatural inward transformation of Sonship takes hold, it overflows into outward responses that shape our daily lives. These Kingdom responses are the natural evidence of a life aligned with the Father's love, revealing His presence through our actions, attitudes, and interactions. Just as a healthy branch produces fruit by abiding in the vine, these responses flow from our connection with the Lord, impacting every moment of our daily lives.

Confidence rises within us as we embrace our identity in Sonship. No longer searching for approval or striving for validation, we move through life with assurance, knowing we are fully loved and chosen. This transforms how we make decisions, approach challenges, and engage with people. In conversations, we speak with clarity and conviction. In uncertain moments, we stand firm rather than shrinking back. Confidence in Sonship allows us to take bold steps into what the Father has called us to do, trusting that He has equipped us for every assignment.

Rest comes naturally, freeing us from anxiety and striving. In a world driven by pressure and performance, living from Sonship allows us to live life from a place of rest, confident that the Father is actively involved in our daily lives.

This daily posture of rest does not mean inactivity but rather a deep trust in His guidance. As we lean into His presence, we navigate our responsibilities from this place of rest, avoiding burnout and embracing a life of joy and purpose. This rest positions us to hear the Father's voice more clearly, discern His leading, and walk in sync with the Holy Spirit.

From rest flows hope—an unshakable expectation of the Father's goodness. Hope transforms how we face our future, keeping our eyes fixed on His promises rather than the limitations of the present. It keeps us anchored in faith and allows us to persist through trials with an unwavering belief that His purposes will unfold in His perfect timing. Hope fills our daily interactions, reshaping our perspective and encouraging those around us. As we live from Sonship, we become carriers of hope, and we invite others to see beyond their circumstances and into the reality of God's faithfulness.

Faith emerges from hope, giving substance to what we believe. It is not blind optimism but a confident trust in the Father's love and His ability to bring His word to pass. Faith shapes our prayers, our choices, and our responses to adversity. It empowers us to take action, whether we are stepping into new opportunities, praying boldly, or standing firm in seasons of uncertainty. Just as Abraham believed in God's promise despite the impossibility of his situation, we live each day with the conviction that the Father is faithful to His word.

As we walk in faith, joy becomes a defining characteristic of our lives. This is not a fleeting emotion but a supernatural work of the Holy Spirit, flowing from the Father's presence. Joy transcends circumstances, anchoring us in His love and filling us with unshakable confidence in His goodness. It sustains us in difficult times and enables us to worship and give thanks even in trials. Like Paul and Silas singing in prison, joy rises above hardship and testifies to the goodness of God. It is a testimony to the world that draws others into the reality of life with Him.

Gratitude flows from joy, shaping our outlook on life. As we recognize the Father's hand in every detail, we cultivate a heart of thanksgiving. Gratitude changes how we speak, how we think, and how we respond to both blessings and challenges. Rather than focusing on what is missing, we live with an awareness of what has already been given. This perspective keeps our hearts tender and responsive to His leading, allowing greater revelation and deeper intimacy with the Father. As we express gratitude, we reflect His goodness and invite others to see His hand at work in their own lives.

All of these responses culminate in love—the ultimate expression of Sonship. Love is the heartbeat of the Kingdom, the defining mark of those who walk with the Father. As we are filled with His love, it overflows into our daily interactions, shaping how we treat people, serve, and extend grace. Love moves us beyond self-centeredness, compelling us to see others through the Father's eyes. It transforms our relationships, fueling acts of kindness, forgiveness, and generosity. Love is not something we manufacture—it is the outflow of a life surrendered to Him, a life that reflects His very nature.

When we live from Sonship, these responses shape how we think, act, and engage with the world. They impact how we approach work, relationships, decision-making, and personal challenges. Confidence gives us the boldness to step into opportunities, rest frees us from striving, hope keeps us anchored, faith believes, joy sustains, gratitude shapes our perspective, and love compels us to action. These responses are not separate aspects of our identity; they are the natural overflow of a life transformed by the Father's love.

As we embrace these responses, they change us and influence the world around us. Our families, workplaces, and communities are transformed as we live as sons and daughters who know who they are. This is the impact of an awakened identity—it doesn't just change our hearts; it changes everything. Every interaction becomes an opportunity to reveal the Father's heart, every challenge a chance to demonstrate faith, and every moment an invitation to bring Heaven to Earth. This is what it means to live in Sonship, carrying His presence into every sphere of life and advancing His Kingdom with every step we take.

A Kingdom Mandate

Sonship is an invitation to step fully into the life we are designed for—a life rooted in the Father's love, empowered by the Holy Spirit, and aligned with His purpose to be conformed to the image of His Son, Jesus. You are created for a relationship with the Father, to experience the fullness of His love and reflect it to the world. Embracing Sonship is not just about knowing who you are; it's about stepping into why you are created—to live as His son or daughter and fulfill His purpose for you.

Jesus becomes our ultimate model of Sonship. He lived in perfect alignment with the Father, carrying these daily realities within Himself and responding to the world out of His unshakable identity as the Son of God. Everything He did—His words, miracles, and interactions—flowed from abiding in the Father's love. He did not strive for validation or act independently of the Father. Instead, He moved in confidence, peace, authority, and joy, demonstrating what it means to live fully as a son. His faith was unwavering, His hope unshakable, and His love boundless. This is the same reality we are invited into—to walk as Jesus walked, living from the fullness of Sonship and responding to the world with the same heart and power.

The inward realities of Sonship—security, peace, confidence, rest, hope, and faith (and more) are the foundation that enables us to live out Kingdom responses. Just as Jesus extended love, grace, and truth to those around Him, we, too, have the capacity to carry these same attributes in our daily lives. His Sonship was evident in the miracles He performed and how He forgave, served, and carried the Father's heart into every encounter. He did nothing apart from the Father, and in the same way, our lives are meant to be an overflow of abiding in Him. As we walk in our identity as sons and daughters, we begin to carry His presence into every sphere of our lives, influencing our families, workplaces, and communities with the tangible love and power of the Father.

Sonship is a shared identity in the household of God that unites us as a family. It is the foundation from which we live fully in His love, growing together, strengthening one another, and carrying His presence into the world. As His sons and daughters, we walk in the fullness of His calling, joined together in purpose and mission. We are His family, formed and shaped to reveal His heart, reflect His love, and advance His Kingdom.

Yet, as a family, we are assigned to fulfill a mandate. This mandate is to make disciples of all nations. Jesus said it clearly in Matthew 6:10, when he said, "Your Kingdom come, Your will be done, on Earth as it is in Heaven." This is where Sonship leads: to fulfilling our assignment to change the world. From Sonship flows the authority, purpose, and unity needed to be Christ's Ekklesia—a people awakened to legislate Heaven on Earth. Sonship positions us to step into our calling, not just as sons and daughters, but as an assembly empowered to bring the Father's will into every sphere of society. As we live from this identity, we move beyond personal transformation into a corporate mandate, carrying His heart, love, and Kingdom into the world, just as Jesus did.

As God's family, we carry a Kingdom assignment—to make disciples of all nations and establish His will on Earth. Sonship is the foundation that leads us into this mission, equipping us with the authority, purpose, and power to advance His Kingdom. From this identity, we step into our calling as Christ's Ekklesia. Sonship and Ekklesia are not separate realities but two expressions of our identity—one relational, one functional. As we embrace our identity as sons and daughters, we step into the adventure of uniting together as His governing body on Earth. This is the natural outflow of living in Sonship, and it is here that our *commission* unfolds as we take our place as Christ's Ekklesia.

SECTION TWO

Ekklesia

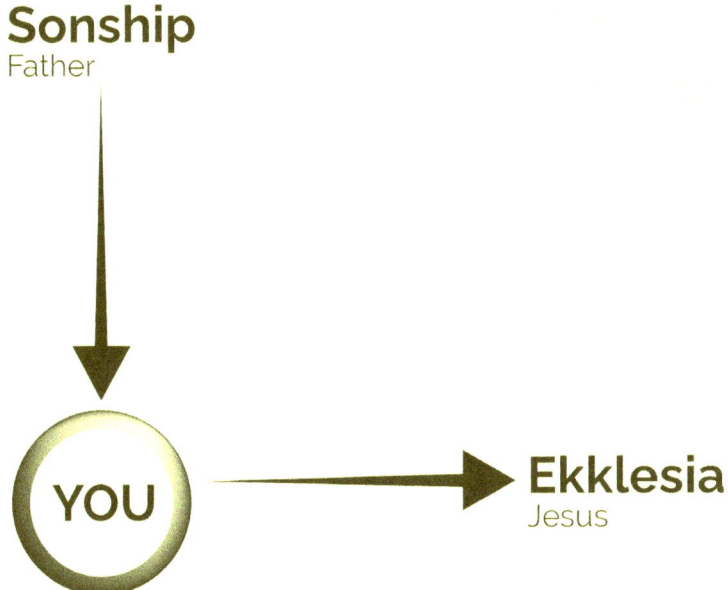

5.
From Sonship to Ekklesia

Our awakening in Christ begins with the profound revelation of our identity as sons and daughters of God, what the New Testament defines as "Sonship." This foundational identity provides us with security, purpose, and the assurance of His unchanging love. We are no longer orphans striving for acceptance or worth; instead, we are welcomed into God's family, overflowing with grace, and granted full rights as His children. This transformation from orphanhood to Sonship is deeply significant. It is not merely about understanding who we are but about experiencing the heart of the Father and His desire for an intimate relationship with us.

However, the revelation of Sonship is merely the starting point of our spiritual formation. While Sonship serves as the bedrock of our identity, it does not fully encompass our mission. Sonship grounds us in our relationship with the Father and propels us toward a greater mission. This mission involves representing our Father on Earth, carrying His authority, and fulfilling His divine purposes. This integration of relational and functional identity is a critical step in our spiritual growth. Just as a child matures and takes on adult responsibilities, we, as sons and daughters of God, are called to step into the authoritative role of the Ekklesia, the governing assembly that Jesus established.

Embracing both our relational and functional identity is a natural progression in our spiritual maturity, an integration that reflects the fullness of Christ. Our relational identity as sons and daughters must be fully embraced and lived out because this secure foundation fuels and empowers our functional identity as the Ekklesia. These are not two separate identities but rather two sides of the same coin, each essential for completing our walk in Christ. Without a solid grasp of our Sonship, our efforts as the Ekklesia could become driven by self-effort and a need for validation or approval, leading to works-based efforts to bring revival. On the other hand, if we do not embrace our role as the Ekklesia, our Sonship remains incomplete, lacking the outward expression of our relational identity.

Both our relational and functional identity are essential to disciple nations and bring about lasting transformation in the world. Our relational identity equips us with understanding our inheritance and the authority we carry as children of God. This identity gives us the confidence to function as the Ekklesia, directing that authority into action and aligning us with Christ's mandate to bring His world into this one. This chapter explores this vital transition, demonstrating how our identity as sons and daughters empowers us to function as the Ekklesia, fulfilling our divine mandate to disciple nations and change the world one person at a time for God's glory.

Doing Church or Becoming Ekklesia

I was taught that the success of a church is often measured by three main factors, which I refer to as the "killer bees": buildings, budgets, and bodies. At nearly every pastor's conference I attended, three questions were almost always asked: What's your name? Where is your church? And how big is it? Many pastors would exaggerate their numbers—something they jokingly call "evangelistically speaking"—to avoid the embarrassment of sharing lower weekly attendance. The underlying belief seems to be that the larger the Sunday morning crowd size, the more successful the church is. But why is that?

What typically comes next is a discussion about the location and design of your church building. How large is it? What's the seating capacity? I quickly learned that both pastors and church members have a deep attachment to their buildings. A board member from a church I previously served once proudly said, "We have the best bathrooms in the entire Assemblies of God!" It speaks to how much we prioritize our buildings. I'm not here to argue that the size of our churches or having adequate facilities for people is inherently wrong, but that these factors alone cannot define the true nature or success of the church.

I want to suggest that, by and large, the church often measures its success by attendance. In many ways, we've placed value on the wrong metrics. It's entirely possible to know how to build a crowd, fill a room, and grow a church yet still have little influence in the community. This happens because we've come to believe—or have been taught—that success is measured by how many people attend our church, the quality of the buildings they gather in, and whether or not we have enough funds to sustain it all.

Because this has become the standard measurement for the church, many pastors feel pressured to offer more programs and events to draw more people into the building, all to drive up attendance to ensure the church's success. I remember reading books on how to break through the barriers of 200,

400, 800, and beyond. While these books can be helpful, they put attendance at the heart of the church's goals. So much of what we do has its means toward this end.

So, the question must be asked: Is this what Jesus had in mind when He said, "I will build my church"?

A 2024 Pew Research Center survey found that 80 percent of U.S. adults believe religion is losing its influence in public life, with nearly half perceiving a growing conflict between their religious beliefs and mainstream culture.[3] While we focus on boosting church attendance, we could be losing our influence in the world. Culture is pressing against the church, pushing us to conform to its image.

What do we do?

This brings to mind the true story of Hendrick Kraemer, a bishop in Denmark during World War II. He described the panic that swept through the clergy of his diocese as the Nazis marched in to occupy their country. As priests and pastors gathered at his home, they anxiously asked, "What shall we do?" Kraemer responded, "First, we must ask who we are. If we know who we are, then we will know what to do."

In a similar way, the church must first focus on understanding its identity before determining its actions. When we truly comprehend who we are, the path forward becomes clear. It all comes down to identity, specifically our functional identity—who we are as the church, and the mission before us.

We must turn to the Word of God and unpack its meaning to grasp this. It all begins with Jesus standing with His disciples in front of the Gates of Hades, declaring that He will build His church.

---

[3] Pew Research Center. (March 15, 2024). "8 in 10 Americans Say Religion Is Losing Influence in Public Life." (Online)

A Revelation at the Gates of Hades

When Jesus first introduced the concept of Ekklesia in Matthew 16:13-19, He chose a setting that was far from ordinary. Jesus and His disciples were in Caesarea Philippi, a region known for its deep involvement in pagan worship and occult practices.

The Gates of Hades, located in this region, was a site known for pagan rituals and had a reputation as a gateway to the underworld. This site is closely linked to the worship of the half-man, half-goat god Pan and 14 other deities and was believed to be a physical and spiritual threshold where the forces of darkness exerted their influence. According to Genesis 6:1-4, it is near this very place, at the foot of Mount Hermon, that the *sons of God* took human wives, leading to the birth of offspring that brought widespread wickedness to the Earth. For the Jews, this location was far more than a center of idol worship; it was ground zero for everything that opposes the Kingdom of God—a place where evil is concentrated and celebrated.

Jesus travels with His disciples for two days from Caesarea Philippi up to the foot of Mount Hermon, standing before the Gates of Hades to release two of the greatest revelations in the New Testament (Matthew 16:13-19). You would assume these revelations would be declared at the temple in Jerusalem—but they are not. They are declared at the Gates of Hades, stunning in it's boldness, and shocking in it's implication. The first is the revelation of who Jesus is, and the second is our assignment that directly flows from that revelation.

When Jesus asked, "Who do you say the Son of Man is?" Simon Peter responded, "You are the Christ, the Son of the living God." This was not only a revelation given by the Father identifying Jesus as the long-awaited Messiah, as incredible as this is, but it also served as a powerful declaration to the spiritual forces of darkness that the King and Deliverer had come to destroy their works and influence on humanity.

Jesus affirmed Peter's declaration by saying, "Upon this rock, I will build My church." In this statement, Jesus declared that He is building something, and it's imperative that we understand exactly what that is. Jesus made it clear that based on the revelation of His identity as the Christ, what He is building is His church. However, it's crucial to recognize that the word Jesus used was not *church* as we commonly understand it today, but "assembly"—the Greek word *Ekklesia*. The terms *church* and *Ekklesia* are not interchangeable; they carry different meanings, which we will discuss momentarily.

The location, timing, and circumstances all emphasize the profound significance of this moment. Jesus, the Son of God, and our long-awaited Messiah, wasn't merely establishing His Ekklesia; He was doing so in the heart of spiritual opposition, boldly declaring that the Gates of Hades would not prevail against it. This declaration was a powerful revelation of Jesus's authority and the authority given to all who follow Him, empowering the assembly, His Ekklesia, to stand firm, actively engage the forces of darkness, and advance God's Kingdom on Earth.

The Foundation of the Ekklesia

In response to Peter's revelation, Jesus revealed that He would build His Ekklesia upon the rock of His identity as the Christ. The *Son* of the living God. The term "Ekklesia" was not a new concept in Jesus's time; it was a well-known term in Roman culture, referring to a legislative assembly or a governing body. However, Jesus infused this term with a new, divine meaning, transcending its original cultural context. He was not speaking of a physical building or a religious institution; instead, He was referring to a called-out assembly, a governing body of believers who would carry out God's will on Earth.

In its original Greek context, the Ekklesia was an assembly of citizens in a city-state responsible for making decisions on matters of public policy, including issues of war, peace, and law. This was not a passive gathering but an active, authoritative body that influenced the direction of society. Jesus's use of this term was intentional and revolutionary. By declaring that He would build His Ekklesia, Jesus established a governing body on Earth composed of sons and daughters, who would have the authority to enact His Father's will, challenge the forces of darkness, and bring His Kingdom to bear in every area of life. This was a significant departure from the traditional understanding of Jewish religious gatherings. The Ekklesia was not a static institution confined to a specific location, but a dynamic, authoritative body positioned to advance the Kingdom of God, even in the face of spiritual opposition.

Jesus emphasized that the Gates of Hades would not prevail against His Ekklesia, highlighting its resolute nature and divine authority. This was not just about engaging in spiritual warfare but about exercising the authority to govern, bind, loose, and make decisions that would have earthly and eternal ramifications.

Jesus's declaration that He would build His Ekklesia was a promise of a powerful, victorious body of believers—a household of sons and daughters carrying out His mission on Earth, just as Jesus did as a Son, fully living out His Sonship in communion with the Father and exercising the authority that came with it.

This Ekklesia would not be confined to a building or limited by human institutions. It would be a global movement, empowered by the Holy Spirit, with the authority to bring God's will to pass in every nation, tribe, and tongue. Understanding the Ekklesia as a governing body is essential to fulfill our mission as Christ's representatives on Earth. It calls us to a higher level of engagement with the world, which goes beyond traditional religious practices and into cultural transformation.

The first time Ekklesia appears in Scripture is when Jesus declares it in Matthew 16:18. The New Testament writers use the Greek word Ekklesia 115 times, and in every instance where we see the word "church," the original word is "Ekklesia." Yet, in all but three instances, it has been translated as "church." This incomplete translation has profoundly reshaped our understanding of what it means to be sons and daughters in this world. Instead of recognizing ourselves as a governing assembly with the authority to legislate the affairs of our cities, states, and nations, we have often reduced "church" to a place of worship and religious activity within the walls of a building.

One translation, however, restores the original intent of Jesus's words. The Passion Translation of Matthew 16:18 captures what He truly declared that day:

> **Matthew 16:18** (TPT) I give you the name Peter, a stone. And this truth of who I am will be the bedrock foundation on which I will build my church—*my legislative assembly*, and the power of death will not be able to overpower it!

Mistaken Identity

The original Ekklesia was intended to be a mobile, mission-driven assembly, but the concept of "church" introduced the idea of a static, location-based institution. This redefinition diluted the original mission of the Ekklesia, shifting the focus from equipping and sending out believers to maintaining buildings, traditions, and programs. The body of Christ, which was meant to be an apostolic, city-taking force, gradually became a pastoral institution focused primarily on caring for the congregation's needs within the confines of a building.

This shift from Ekklesia to "church" reflects a profound loss of identity and purpose. The Ekklesia was called to be a transformative force in culture that challenged the status quo, confronted injustice, and brought the light of Christ into the darkest places. However, as the church became more institutionalized, the focus shifted from advancing the Kingdom of God to preserving religious traditions, maintaining structures, and providing spiritual services to the faithful. Though these things have an important role in the believer's life, the dynamic, missional nature of the Ekklesia was lost, and with it, the sense of urgency and authority to disciple nations and transform culture.

As a result, the church became a place where people went to receive equipping and care—both valuable—but we lost sight of its true purpose as a movement actively engaging the world with the gospel. This inward focus led to a long-lasting shift in the mission of the body of Christ. Instead of seeing themselves as part of a governing assembly with the authority to bring God's Kingdom to Earth, many Christians began to view their faith as a personal and private matter, disconnected from the broader mission of discipling nations.

This misunderstanding of identity has created a disconnect between our calling as sons and daughters of God and our mission as the Ekklesia. To reclaim our true identity and fulfill our mission, we must return to the original understanding of the Ekklesia as a governing body called to bring God's will into every area of life. This means recognizing that our role as the Ekklesia is not limited to what happens within the walls of a church building but extends to every sphere of society—government, education, business, media, arts, and family. It requires a revolution in our thinking from seeing ourselves as merely members of a religious institution to understanding our identity as active participants in a Spirit-led legislative assembly with the authority to shape and change the world for His glory.

Evolution of "Church"

The transition from Ekklesia to "church" was not an abrupt change but instead, a gradual process influenced by historical events, cultural shifts, and theological developments that span several centuries. Understanding this evolution is crucial for grasping why the body of Christ has often struggled with its identity and mission.

In the church's early days, Christ's followers faced severe persecution. The Jewish Sanhedrin and Roman Empire viewed this new movement as a direct threat to its religious and social order. Despite their intense opposition, the early Ekklesia thrived, spreading rapidly worldwide. These early believers had no concept of a "church" paradigm as we know it today—it simply did not exist. They understood their identity as the Ekklesia—called out by God, equipped with authority, and commissioned to advance the Kingdom. They met in homes, public spaces, and wherever they could gather, often under the threat of death. Their mission was clear: to bring the Gospel message to every person and to expand the influence of God's Kingdom, even in the face of persecution.

However, everything began to change in AD 313 when the Roman Emperor Constantine issued the Edict of Milan, granting religious tolerance to Christians. Suddenly, the once-persecuted Ekklesia found favor with the state. Though its sincerity is debated, Constantine's conversion to Christianity and subsequent endorsement of the faith marked the beginning of the church's institutionalization. This shift had significant implications for the identity and mission of the Ekklesia.

As Christianity became more accepted and eventually the official religion of the Roman Empire, the Ekklesia began to take on the characteristics of the surrounding culture. The simplicity and mobility of early gatherings gave way to more formalized worship practices, and the construction of dedicated church buildings became common. These structures were often modeled after Roman basilicas, public buildings used for legal and other civic proceedings. The adoption of these architectural styles further reinforced the idea of the church as a physical location, a place where religious activities occurred, rather than a dynamic, mission-driven assembly.

In the fifth and sixth centuries, the Old English words *cirice* or *cyrice* were starting to be used by the Anglo-Saxon people to refer to church buildings. As Christianity spread across England, the use of *cirice* or *cyrice* to describe the structures where Christians gathered for worship became more common, gradually solidifying their place in the English language.

In 1382, John Wycliffe, an Oxford professor, completed the first handwritten English translation of the Bible from Jerome's Latin text. This translation played a crucial role in popularizing the word "chirche," which Wycliffe used to translate the Latin term "ecclesia." Through Wycliffe's efforts, "chirche" became widely recognized and eventually evolved into the English word "church" used today.

The Protestant Reformation in the 16th century brought a renewed focus on the Scriptures. It sought to correct many of the abuses and errors that had crept into the "church" over the centuries. Reformers like Martin Luther, John Calvin, and William

Tyndale emphasized the importance of returning to the original languages of the Bible to better understand its meaning. In his 1526 translation of the New Testament, Tyndale deliberately chose to translate "Ekklesia" as "congregation" rather than "church," reflecting a return to the idea of a called-out assembly rather than a building.

However, Tyndale's translation met fierce opposition from the established church elite, which saw it as a threat to its authority and power. Tyndale was eventually declared a heretic and executed for his work. His translation, the Tyndale Bible, laid the groundwork for future English versions of the Bible, including the King James Version. Unfortunately, the King James translators reverted to using the term "church," largely due to political and religious pressures, including King James's directive to maintain ecclesiastical terms that supported the hierarchical structure of the Church of England.

As a result, the idea of "church" as a building or institution became deeply ingrained in the English-speaking world, and the true meaning of Ekklesia as a governing, legislative assembly was largely lost. This shift had profound implications for how Christians understood their role in the world. The focus moved away from being an active, mission-focused body engaged in cultural transformation to becoming a more passive, inward-looking institution focused on preserving tradition and religious observance.

Incomplete Reform

The Protestant Reformation was a pivotal moment in church history. It challenged the authority of the Roman Catholic Church and sparked a movement of religious decentralization and justification by faith. Yet, even as the Reformation sought to return to biblical foundations, the concept of the church as an institution remained largely unchallenged.

Reformers like Luther and Calvin addressed many doctrinal issues, but they did not see Tyndale's emphasis on the original understanding of the Ekklesia as significant, and as a result, its true meaning was lost. The church buildings remained central to worship, and hierarchical structures dominated church governance. The idea of the church as a gathering place persisted, shaping the development of Protestant denominations.

While essential, the focus on personal salvation and individual faith often led to a more inward-focused Christianity, where the cultural role of the Ekklesia was diminished. The church became a place to retreat from the world rather than a movement to engage and transform it. This shift contributed to the secularization of society, as the church increasingly withdrew from public life and cultural influence.

In the modern era, this secularization of society has resulted in a significant identity crisis within the church. Many Christians struggle to reconcile their personal faith with the broader mission of the Ekklesia. The idea of the church as a static, institutional entity has often led to a disconnect between Sunday worship and the rest of life. The original mandate to disciple nations and transform culture has been overshadowed by a focus on maintaining religious programs and practices within the walls of the church building.

It's imperative that we reclaim the original vision of the Ekklesia, recognizing that this is what Jesus is building. The *church* is not just a place or an institution, but a people called out by God to govern, influence, and bring about His Kingdom on Earth. This resurgence of the Ekklesia calls us as sons and daughters to *awaken* to our functional identity and mission, challenging us to step into our God-given authority to disciple nations and transform culture.

What, Then, Is the Ekklesia?

The term *Ekklesia* originated in the Grecian Empire around 400 BC as a governmental assembly where citizens gathered to legislate, govern, and influence the affairs of their city-states. It was a foundational institution in the democratic city-states of Greece. When Rome conquered Greece, it adopted and adapted the Ekklesia into its imperial system, using it to manage city affairs and as a tool for cultural transformation. As the Roman Empire expanded, Ekklesias were established in newly conquered territories to enforce Roman law and shape these cities to reflect Rome itself. These assemblies held legislative authority, making decisions on public policy and ensuring that Roman governance and culture took root in every region under its rule.

Ekklesia gatherings were not passive; they were active assemblies that shaped cities and influenced culture. When Jesus declared, "I will build *my* Ekklesia," He intentionally chose a term describing His governing body with the authority to enact His Father's will on Earth. This was not merely about gathering believers for worship on a Sunday morning but establishing an assembly of His sons and daughters to disciple nations, change the world, and bring Heaven to Earth as He did.

To function as the Ekklesia, we must deepen our ongoing and life-giving communion with the Father through prayer, worship, and the Word of God. This communion is not merely a means to grow our churches but the foundation for carrying out the Great Commission.

In the next chapter, we will delve deeper into the biblical and historical context of the Ekklesia, exploring why Jesus chose the Ekklesia and how the early church embraced this functional identity to transform the world, turning the world *upside down*. Understanding these aspects will equip us to awaken and reclaim our functional identity and mission as Christ's Ekklesia in the modern world.

6.
The Original Operating System

On the day of Pentecost, a sound from heaven, like a mighty rushing wind, filled the room where they were sitting, ushering in the Spirit of God with power the room could hardly contain. In that moment, everything changed. The disciples were no longer just followers of Jesus; they became vessels of His very presence. This was the birth of something unlike anything the world had ever seen—not an institution, not a building-centered religion, but the *Ekklesia*. As noted earlier, the early believers had no concept of a "church" as we know it today; they only understood *Ekklesia*—a governing legislative assembly called out to advance God's Kingdom on Earth. To truly grasp the Book of Acts, we must read it through this lens, recognizing that the early church functioned exclusively as Christ's Ekklesia: sons and daughters carrying His authority, power, and love into the world around them, driving out darkness with light.

Imagine it: ordinary men and women—fishermen, tax collectors, former zealots, and others who had walked with Jesus—were now infused with His purpose and power. They spoke in tongues, languages they had never learned, declaring God's wonders in words that confounded those around them. When Peter, stood to preach, thousands were cut to the heart, and received the Lord. It was as if Heaven had opened, and the Spirit was supernaturally drawing people into the Kingdom.

This was not merely an event but an invasion of God's presence into ordinary lives, transforming them into extraordinary carriers of His love and power. The Ekklesia—the called-out assembly of God's people—no longer questioned or hesitated; they moved with a boldness ignited by the Spirit. Miracles became part of their daily lives—people were healed, demons were cast out, and even the shadow of Peter brought healing to the sick. The oppressed were set free, the dead were raised to life, and angels broke them out of prison, it was as if Heaven itself refused to be restrained. These men and women were not just participants but God's chosen representatives on Earth, bearers of a divine authority that could not be contained.

This was the Ekklesia—the original design for God's people, not a structure or a ritual but a living, breathing movement. It was God's operating system, empowering believers to bring His light wherever they went. In this Ekklesia, every person had a place, every heart had a role, and every voice carried the authority of Heaven itself. They were a family, a movement, and a force that changed the course of history, and nothing could stop them.

Strategic Departure from Religious Norms

When Jesus declared in Matthew 16:18, "I will build my church (*ekklesia*), and the gates of Hades will not overcome it," He wasn't introducing a religious term. Instead, He unveiled His plan using a well-known governmental concept familiar to His disciples. This plan was to establish a governmental operating system with the authority to disciple nations and change the world—the Ekklesia.

To grasp the significance of Jesus's choice of the word Ekklesia, we must first understand the context of His time. The Jewish religious landscape was dominated by two primary institutions: the temple and the synagogue. The Temple in Jerusalem was the epicenter of Jewish worship for centuries, where sacrifices were made, and God's presence was believed to dwell. The Synagogue, found in every Jewish community, is where scripture was read, and prayers were made as people gathered. Both institutions were deeply rooted in Jewish tradition and held significant sway over the religious and social life of the people.

Given these well-established institutions, it would have been logical for Jesus to align His movement with the Temple or the Synagogue. Yet, He did neither. Instead, He chose the Ekklesia—a concept borrowed from the Greco-Roman world that had little to do with religion and everything to do with government and societal influence.

Jesus's declaration of building "My Ekklesia" was a significant and distinct statement, as He was not merely using a familiar term but redefining it with a profound new purpose. By choosing this term, He set His Ekklesia apart from all others, establishing it as a unique assembly with a divine mandate, different from the traditional civic assemblies that governed their cities.

While, as mentioned earlier, the disciples knew exactly what the Ekklesia was—a governing, legislative assembly with real authority—they didn't yet understand how they could possibly function as one. Fishermen, tax collectors, zealots—how could Jesus expect them to operate as a governing body? No wonder they assumed He was planning to overthrow Rome and establish a political kingdom. But Jesus was establishing His government—one far greater than they imagined. He wasn't overthrowing Rome; He was inaugurating a spiritual kingdom, one that would overthrow the rule of hell itself!

Jesus was calling them to be a spiritual Ekklesia. That's why, in Matthew 16:18, He declared His Ekklesia not at the Temple in Jerusalem, the center of religious activity, but at the gates of Hades—the center of demonic strongholds in Caesarea Philippi. This choice was intentional. By selecting this location, Jesus made it unmistakably clear that His Ekklesia was not about religious or civil authority alone, but about something far greater—a mandate to confront and overthrow the very gates of Hades, standing boldly against spiritual strongholds and the powers of darkness.

By choosing the term Ekklesia, Jesus made it clear that His Kingdom would go beyond the confines of the walls of religion, establishing a movement designed to influence every part of society—government, education, family, business, media, and more. This means Christians are to engage in politics to promote justice, shape education with godly principles, lead businesses with integrity, and use media to proclaim biblical truth and values.

As a result, they would legislate Kingdom principles and values, bringing transformation to every corner of the world and reshaping cultures according to God's divine purpose. Through His Ekklesia, Jesus envisioned a dynamic community of believers who would actively partner with him to bring His Kingdom into every corner of the world in tangible, life-changing ways.

Assembly, Not Building

The question then arises: Why didn't Jesus choose the Temple or the Synagogue as the foundation for His movement?

These were, after all, the established centers of religious life in Israel.

The Temple, with all its grandeur and religious significance, had long been regarded by the Jewish people as the dwelling place of God. However, it was tied to a specific location and was ultimately destroyed in AD 70, just 37 years after Jesus's resurrection. The Temple's centrality in Jewish worship also meant that it was inherently exclusive—only Jews could fully participate in its rituals, and even within the Jewish community, access was restricted by various laws and regulations.

While more accessible and widespread, the synagogue was still limited by its reliance on buildings and formal gatherings. It was a place for reading scripture and prayer but lacked the mobility and flexibility necessary to expand the Kingdom of God. Unforeseen then, the gospel was to make its way to the Gentile world, which had limited knowledge and participation in Jewish synagogues.

It's important to note that although the traditional religious structures were no longer the focal point of the Ekklesia, the essential elements—such as the presence of God, the authority of scripture, the practice of prayer, and the value of fellowship and more—were not abandoned but were instead carried over and integrated into the life of the Ekklesia. These foundational practices remained central, not as rigid structures, but as life-giving practices that would sustain and empower the Ekklesia in its mission to engage with and transform every sphere of society. The shift was not away from these spiritual pillars but toward a more expansive expression of them, where they would infuse every aspect of life through the person and work of the Holy Spirit, guiding and shaping the Ekklesia as it carried out its Kingdom mandate in the world.

The Ekklesia was not confined to a single location or bound by a rigid structure. The disciples carried out Jesus's mission, preaching the gospel, healing the sick, and establishing the Ekklesia wherever they went—in homes, marketplaces, and even prisons. It was built on relationships, not programs. It was a community of people, not a physical place. This made it the ideal structure for a movement to reach every tribe, tongue, and nation.

Moreover, the Ekklesia was designed to transform public life like salt, light, and leaven. Unlike the Temple and Synagogue, primarily concerned with religious matters, the Ekklesia was inherently involved in legislating cultural and societal transformation through prayer, power, and serving others. It was equipping His followers to influence culture, and the Ekklesia was the operating system through which His Kingdom would advance.

A Kingdom Movement

The choice of the Ekklesia also reflects Jesus's broader mission to establish the Kingdom of God on Earth. His teachings were filled with references to the Kingdom—He spoke of it more than anything else. The Kingdom of God was not a distant, otherworldly concept; it was a present reality that Jesus brought into the world through His life, death, and resurrection.

The Ekklesia was the vehicle for this Kingdom movement. It was not just a gathering of believers for worship and teaching; it was an assembly with the authority to legislate and govern according to the values of the Kingdom. The Ekklesia was to be Jesus's hands and feet in the world, carrying out His mission to seek and save that which was lost, bring justice and mercy, and demonstrate the love and power of God in tangible ways.

This was a radical departure from the religious structures of the time. The Temple and Synagogue focused on maintaining religious purity and tradition, with leaders more concerned about upholding rituals rather than engaging the broader culture. In contrast, the Ekklesia was concerned with advancing the Kingdom of God in the world. It was outward-focused, mission-driven, and empowered by the Holy Spirit to carry out its task.

Jesus's decision to establish His Kingdom through the Ekklesia ensured His movement would not be limited to a single culture or people group like the Temple and Synagogue, which were deeply intertwined with Jewish identity and culture. The Ekklesia transcended cultural and ethnic boundaries. Everyone from a Roman centurion to a prostitute to a Pharisee, slave, and even a Samaritan could be a part of the Kingdom of God and thus a member of the Ekklesia.

The Ekklesia differed distinctly from the prevailing religious structures in its flexibility and adaptability. Unlike the Temple, which was tied to Jerusalem, or the Synagogue, which required specific rituals and practices, the Ekklesia could thrive in any environment. The disciples preached and taught in public squares, homes, in lecture halls, marketplaces, and while imprisoned, establishing Ekklesias regardless of their circumstances.

As a result, the revival epicenter eventually shifted from Jerusalem to Antioch, where the gospel took root and spread northward, reaching as far as Rome and beyond. This transition marked a pivotal moment—the movement was no longer centered in one location but was advancing dynamically, carried by those who embraced their role as Christ's "legislative assembly."

Another critical reason Jesus chose the Ekklesia was its reliance on the power of the Holy Spirit. The Ekklesia was not just a human institution; it was a divine assembly empowered by

God to carry out His mission on Earth. Jesus knew His followers would face opposition, persecution, and the challenges of spreading the Gospel across different cultures and nations. They would need more than human wisdom and strength; they would need the supernatural power of the Holy Spirit.

This reliance on the Holy Spirit set the Ekklesia apart from the Temple and Synagogue. While the Temple was the place where God's presence was believed to dwell, the Ekklesia was the assembly where God's Spirit actively moved and worked in and through His people, empowering them to preach the Gospel, heal the sick, cast out demons, and perform miracles. The Ekklesia was a dynamic, Spirit-filled community that carried the presence and power of God into the world.

A Narrative of Transformation

The Book of Acts provides a powerful narrative of how the early believers embodied the Ekklesia in their daily lives. From the moment the Holy Spirit descended upon them at Pentecost, the followers of Jesus began to live out the reality of the Ekklesia in ways that were both extraordinary and deeply rooted in the ordinary rhythms of life.

The early believers didn't see themselves as part of a new religion but as participants in a Kingdom movement. As previously established, they had no concept of church as we understand it today. Instead, they were Christ's Ekklesia—a way of life infused with God's presence and power.

Pentecost: The Birth of the Ekklesia

Peter, once a fisherman with little formal education, stood on the day of Pentecost and delivered a sermon that pierced the hearts of those who listened. With boldness, he proclaimed the death and resurrection of Jesus, calling the people to repentance and baptism. That day, about 3,000 people were saved and added to their number (Acts 2:41)—a powerful demonstration of the Holy Spirit working through the Ekklesia.

This was not the birth of a new religion but the awakening of their functional identity, empowered to change the world. The Ekklesia was not confined to a building or just weekly gatherings; it was a living, breathing community that met both in the temple courts and in homes. The community devoted itself to the apostles' teaching, to fellowship, to the breaking of bread, and prayer. This devotion created a vibrant, Spirit-filled community where signs and wonders were common, and the needs of all were met through radical generosity.

Living Out the Ekklesia Paradigm

As the Ekklesia grew, it began to attract attention—not just from those being saved but also from the religious and political authorities of the day. The healing of a lame man by Peter and John in Acts 3 was a powerful demonstration of the Ekklesia's authority and power. It was followed by courageous preaching that led to further conversions but also brought about persecution from the religious elite. Peter and John were arrested, yet even in the face of threats, they continued to proclaim the name of Jesus with boldness.

The believers' understanding of themselves as the Ekklesia meant that they were constantly engaged in the work of the Kingdom. Whether gathering for prayer, sharing meals, or preaching in the streets, they saw themselves as a governing assembly called to bring the reality of God's Kingdom into every area of life. This was not a passive faith but an active, engaged, and empowered way of living that sought to transform the world around them.

The early Ekklesia was characterized by its openness to all who sought salvation. In Acts 10, Peter received a vision that challenged his understanding of Jewish purity laws, instructing him to eat animals considered unclean. This symbolic act prepared him for encountering Cornelius, a Roman centurion. Through this experience, the Lord revealed that the Gospel was now extended to the Gentiles. When Peter preached the Gospel to Cornelius and his household, they believed in Jesus and received the Holy Spirit just as the Jewish believers had at Pentecost, confirming that the Gospel was for everyone, regardless of social or ethnic background.

The inclusion of the Gentiles was a significant moment in the history of the Ekklesia. It marked the breaking down of the barriers that had separated Jews and Gentiles for centuries. The Gospel, carried out by the Ekklesia, was now clearly a global movement, not confined to one nation, building, or ethnicity, but open to all who would receive the message of Jesus.

Beyond Persecution

Stephen's martyrdom in Acts 7 began a wave of persecution that scattered the Ekklesia throughout Judea and Samaria. Yet, what seemed like a setback was a strategic move in God's plan. As the believers were scattered, they carried the message of the Kingdom with them, forming new Ekklesias in every town and city they entered.

One of the key figures in this expansion was Philip, who traveled to Samaria and preached the Gospel with great success. The Samaritans, considered outsiders by the Jews, received the message joyfully, and many were baptized. Philip's encounter with the Ethiopian eunuch further demonstrated the Ekklesia's expanding reach as the Gospel began to spread beyond the borders of Judea and into the Gentile world.

Meanwhile, in Acts 9, the most unlikely of conversions took place. Saul, a fierce persecutor of the Ekklesia, encountered the risen Jesus on the road to Damascus. Blinded and humbled, Saul became Paul, one of the early Ekklesia's most passionate and influential leaders. His conversion marked a turning point, as he would go on to take the Gospel to the Gentiles, planting Ekklesias throughout the Roman Empire.

Paul's missionary travels, recorded in the latter chapters of Acts, took him across the Roman Empire, where he planted Ekklesias in cities like Philippi, Corinth, Ephesus, and Rome. These trips were marked by both great successes and significant challenges, including persecution, imprisonment, and opposition from both Jews and Gentiles.

Paul's letters, which form a significant portion of the New Testament, provide valuable insights into the life and challenges of the early Ekklesia. These letters reveal the Ekklesia as a dynamic, Spirit-filled community that was deeply committed to glorifying Jesus and living out the reality of the Kingdom in every aspect of life. Paul's teachings on unity, spiritual gifts, leadership, and moral purity helped shape the identity and mission of the Ekklesia in its formative years.

Despite his challenges, Paul remained steadfast in his mission to proclaim the Gospel and establish Ekklesias wherever he went. His apostolic work demonstrates the global nature of the Ekklesia and the expansive vision that Jesus had for His movement. The Ekklesia was not confined to one location or culture; it was a universal movement that transcended all boundaries and brought the message of the Kingdom to every corner of the Earth.

A Modern-Day Ekklesia Movement

The Jesus Movement of the 1960s and 1970s was a modern-day resurgence of God's original operating system, the Ekklesia. Amid a cultural upheaval, young people desperately searched for meaning, and many found it in Jesus. This revival didn't conform to institutional expectations or confine itself within church walls. Instead, it echoed the early Ekklesia—uncontainable, Spirit-filled, and overflowing into all areas of life. These new believers were not joining a religion but stepping into a living, breathing assembly empowered by the Holy Spirit. They became carriers of His presence, bringing the message and power of the Kingdom into everyday life.

Gatherings erupted on beaches, in coffeehouses, and in the streets—places where people from all walks of life encountered the presence of God in a raw, authentic way. Like the original Ekklesia, which gathered in homes and public squares, this movement was defined by its organic, relational foundation. The people didn't just preach about Jesus; they embodied His life and teachings in a way that ignited hearts and changed lives. Their influence flowed into every sphere of society, infusing culture with Kingdom values without the approval of religious systems.

This movement was a powerful reminder that the Ekklesia is not a building but a people—sons and daughters walking in their Kingdom identity, standing as a bold, transformative presence in the world. Just as the early Ekklesia was a force that shaped cities and shifted cultures, the Jesus Movement became a conduit for Heaven's invasion on Earth, reclaiming God's purpose for the Ekklesia as a Kingdom-driven, culture-transforming movement. Through it, we're reminded that while buildings and programs serve a purpose, the heart of God's original design has always been about carrying His light and authority wherever we go, bringing revival beyond the church walls.

Can you see how Christ's Ekklesia continues to disrupt norms, break through boundaries, and draw society back to the core of His Kingdom's purpose? It calls for every believer and congregation to embrace God's original operating system as the Ekklesia today, empowered by the Spirit of God, carrying His Kingdom's light into every area of daily life. In this way, we fulfill the vision Jesus spoke in Matthew 16:18: to be a people called out, awakened to His presence, and commissioned to transform our world, legislating Heaven to Earth.

Reclaiming Our Functional Identity

Reflecting on the early Ekklesia, it's clear that what Jesus established was far more than a religious institution. The Ekklesia was a movement—an assembly of called-out ones. It was a living, breathing community of believers deeply committed to following Jesus, making His Kingdom known, and discipling nations. They didn't *go to church*, because they were the Ekklesia.

We long to return to the power and impact of the book of Acts, but in many ways, we've installed the wrong operating system yet are expecting the same results. No matter how much we tweak or upgrade it, a system designed primarily for *church* will never fully produce the movement Jesus intended.

The early church functioned as the Ekklesia—a governing body of sons and daughters called to advance God's Kingdom—yet today, many are trying to replicate its impact while operating within a model that is largely pastoral rather than apostolic, emphasizing caring and gathering more than governing and sending. While pastoring is essential, the Ekklesia was never meant to exist solely for the care of its people but to equip and commission them to bring Kingdom transformation into the world.

The Ekklesia was not about preserving traditions or protecting a religious structure—it was a 24/7 movement, empowered by the Holy Spirit to confront darkness, bring citywide transformation, and establish God's Kingdom on Earth. Until we restore this operating system, we will continue to experience system failures in our efforts to bring lasting revival.

Wherever two or three gathered in His name, the Ekklesia was convened—not confined to a single location but manifesting wherever believers came together. The Book of Acts reveals that the Ekklesia met regularly for teaching, equipping, prayer, and shared meals, strengthening one another in the faith. Tables became pulpits, and everyday life became infused with the supernatural. They functioned as a prophetic community, fully operating in the gifts of the Spirit and walking in step with His guidance. Despite constant persecution, the gospel was preached and the Kingdom continued advancing as the Ekklesia multiplied, demonstrating that the church was not merely a place but a people, *living stones* (1 Peter 2:5), empowered to transform the world.

We must step into and begin living out our functional identity as Christ's Ekklesia, just as the early church did in the Book of Acts. This isn't about abandoning buildings or gatherings but about stepping beyond the walls to engage the world in meaningful, transformative ways. The first believers didn't limit their faith to meetings; they carried the power and authority of the Kingdom into every part of culture. They preached the gospel, healed the sick, and turned the world upside down. When we fully embrace our functional identity as Christ's Ekklesia, we are restored to walk in its true mandate and awakened to its purpose—advancing His Kingdom in the same way the early church did.

7.
Restoring the Church as the Ekklesia

In Matthew 16:19, Jesus said:

> I will give you the keys of the Kingdom of Heaven; whatever you bind on earth will be bound in Heaven, and whatever you loose on Earth will be loosed in Heaven.

This was not just a promise—it was a commissioning. Jesus was equipping His Ekklesia with offensive weapons to confront and overcome the Gates of Hades. The church was never meant to be passive or defensive, merely holding ground. Instead, it was called to advance, to break through enemy strongholds, and to enforce Heaven's agenda on Earth.

To restore the church to its intended purpose, we must reclaim our God-given authority and learn to wield the weapons Jesus entrusted to us. Only then can we effectively advance His Kingdom, establish His rule, and bring transformation to the world around us. And at the center of these weapons are the Kingdom keys—divine authority given to us to bind, loose, and shift the spiritual atmosphere, unlocking God's will on Earth as it is in Heaven.

Offensive Weapons

Jesus's declaration in Matthew 16:19 forms the foundation for understanding the role of the Ekklesia. The "keys of the Kingdom" symbolize both authority and access, granting the Ekklesia the power to bind and loose on Earth with the support of Heaven. This authority is aimed directly at the Gates of Hades, which represent the forces of darkness that seek to keep humanity in bondage.

Revelation 1:18 reveals that Jesus now holds the keys of death and Hades, meaning that Satan stands behind gates to which he no longer holds the keys. Empowered by Christ, the Ekklesia now has access to these gates, allowing us to advance and reclaim territory once dominated by darkness and oppression.

The "Gates of Hades" is often misunderstood. In the context of Jesus's statement, they represent the domain of death and the underworld, the strongholds of Satan. In Greek culture, Hades was considered the realm of the dead, ruled by a powerful deity. Yet Jesus's victory over death and His resurrection marked the ultimate defeat of Hades. Now, He commissions the Ekklesia to confront and dismantle these strongholds.

In ancient cities, gates were not just physical barriers but centers of power where decisions were made and control was exercised. In biblical times, the gates of a city were where elders sat, judgments were made, and leaders conducted business. Gates, therefore, symbolized authority and control. By referring to the Gates of Hades, Jesus emphasized the spiritual and cultural strongholds the Ekklesia must confront. These gates are entry and exit points, and the Ekklesia's task is to release those held captive by darkness and prevent the further encroachment of evil.

In today's world, the gates we face are the ideologies, systems, and structures that stand against God's Kingdom. Think about the cultural strongholds of materialism, secularism, and moral relativism. They dominate public discourse and shape societal values. They are championed in our schools and politics. These gates are trying to close humanity off from the grace of God and make the Earth as dark as hell itself.

The role of the Ekklesia is to challenge these gates, not with physical force, but through spiritual authority, truth, and love. The Ekklesia challenges materialism by calling people to store up treasures in Heaven and embody generosity in a culture consumed by greed; it confronts secularism by boldly proclaiming biblical truth in spaces where God is often silenced, and it opposes moral relativism by standing firmly on the unchanging truth of God's Word in a world that seeks to redefine right and wrong, what's true and what isn't.

In ancient times, the one who held the keys had the power to open and close gates, granting or denying access, so keys symbolize authority and responsibility. When Jesus provides the keys to the Ekklesia, He empowers us to take decisive action in the spiritual realm. This includes binding the works of the enemy and loosing the will of God on Earth.

Just as turning on a light in a dark room immediately dispels the darkness, when we loose the Kingdom—through prayer, faith, and action—peace, healing, and justice naturally follow, and the forces of darkness are automatically bound. It's not about striving to push back the darkness but about exercising the authority given by Jesus to release the light of His Kingdom, knowing that when the light comes, darkness has no choice but to flee. This shifts our focus from battling evil to actively releasing the transformative power of God's presence in both the spiritual and physical realms through Kingdom keys.

When the Ekklesia prays for healing, God's power flows into a person's life. It binds sickness and disease, breaking their hold, and releases wholeness. When leading someone into forgiveness, it looses them from bitterness, setting them free and aligning them with Heaven's will for restoration.

The same principle applies beyond individual lives. When the Ekklesia prays for God's values to be restored in schools and actively participates—whether by speaking up at school board meetings or engaging with educators—it looses the Kingdom of God to operate in that environment. In politics, rather than simply condemning corruption, the Ekklesia is called to bind injustice and loose God's righteousness by voting for leaders who uphold biblical values, advocating for godly policies, and influencing culture with truth.

The Call to Disciple and Baptize Nations

The Great Commission in Matthew 28:19-20 mandates the Ekklesia to disciple nations. This is about transforming entire cultures and societies according to the principles of God's Kingdom. Discipling nations means bringing Jesus's teachings into every sphere of society, including government, education, business, media, arts, entertainment, and family. The Ekklesia is called to influence these areas, ensuring that the values and principles of the Kingdom of God are initiated and upheld.

Discipling nations begins with transforming individuals but doesn't stop there—it extends to influencing systems and structures. In the late 1700s, William Wilberforce, driven by his deep conviction of the injustice of slavery, used his position in England's House of Commons to fight against it. For 15 years, he fought tirelessly against overwhelming odds until the slave trade was abolished. Then, he fought another 13 years for those still enslaved. He and those whom God gathered around him brought freedom to countless people and wiped the stain of slavery from the heart of the English nation.

As the Ekklesia, we, too, are called to be the salt and light in the world, preserving what is good and illuminating the truth. This requires strategic engagement in the cultural, political, and social arenas, where the values of the Kingdom can be established and maintained. Believers shape the education system by promoting godly values, influencing government structures through advocacy for justice and righteousness, and guiding businesses toward ethical practices that serve people and communities.

Today, discipling nations may involve protecting the unborn, feeding and clothing the homeless, speaking out against unethical business practices, voting with our dollars, doing right whether it's profitable or not, ensuring public education reflects Kingdom values, and upholding biblical morality. It means engaging with culture, not withdrawing from it, and using our influence to shape society according to God's will.

Another key practice in discipling nations is baptism. Far more than a religious ritual, baptism represents a deep identification with the life, death, and resurrection of Jesus. It marks a profound transition for individuals and nations as they are immersed in the reality of God's Kingdom. To baptize nations is to bring them under the authority and influence of the Father, Son, and Holy Spirit, initiating a process of lasting transformation.

In ancient Greek literature, the transformation of a cucumber into a pickle illustrates the power of baptism. First, the cucumber is briefly dipped (bapto) to cleanse its surface, preparing it for the process ahead. But this alone doesn't bring change. True transformation happens through ongoing immersion (baptizo) in a brine—a salty, preserving solution—that permeates and permanently alters its nature.

In the same way, the Ekklesia is called not merely to introduce the Gospel but to immerse nations in the Word of God, permeating and permanently transforming lives aligned with the Kingdom of God until cultural, legal, and societal norms reflect Kingdom values. This could involve advocating for biblical values in our education system, such as instilling moral uprightness and cultivating respect for teachers and peers. It also means promoting family unity through principles of forgiveness and reconciliation and ensuring fair business practices that uphold honesty and generosity. As biblical values permeate society, they reshape culture, foster justice, and inspire a way of life rooted in God's love, truth, and righteousness, building a foundation aligned with His Kingdom.

Reinstalling the Original Operating System

The modern church has, in many ways, drifted from its original purpose as the Ekklesia, focusing more on internal programs and maintaining traditions rather than bringing Kingdom influence beyond its walls. Instead of influencing culture and shaping nations, the church often remains insulated within its walls, missing the call to bring Kingdom values into the public square.

To restore the church to its rightful place, we must consider "reinstalling" the operating system Jesus originally designed to disciple nations and change the world. This involves stripping away the cultural and traditional layers accumulated over centuries and returning to the foundational principles laid out by Jesus.

Returning to this original operating system isn't about tweaking a few practices or introducing new programs. It requires a more profound shift that redefines how we see our functional identity and purpose. As Jesus envisioned, the Ekklesia was never meant to be confined to a building or reduced to religious practices and programs alone. Instead, it was designed as a dynamic, empowered assembly with a clear mission to bring God's Kingdom to Earth.

To return to this original operating system, the church must rediscover its role as an active agent of transformation—not just for individuals but for entire cultures and societies. This involves breaking free from the passive mindset that views the church primarily as a place for attending services or receiving ministry. Instead, the church must reawaken. As the hands and feet of Jesus, we are sent out to disciple nations to tackle the spiritual and societal issues that prevent God's Kingdom from flourishing. This means letting go of the unnecessary layers of tradition and bureaucracy that have slowed down the church's mission and focusing again on the powerful simplicity of the design Jesus left us: a Spirit-led, Kingdom-minded, world-changing Ekklesia.

This return to basics invites every believer to see themselves not merely as church attenders but as world changers—people who are called to bring God's Kingdom into every sphere of society. Reinstalling this original system empowers the church to rise again as the transformative force it was always meant to be. It restores our authority as God's people, advancing His Kingdom with renewed conviction and purpose, and equipping us to disciple nations and change the world.

The first step in this process is to reassess our current practices and priorities. Are our church activities truly equipping believers to fulfill their mission? Or have they become focused on maintaining traditions at the expense of advancing the Kingdom of God? Is the Gospel being preached, and are people coming to Christ beyond the walls of the church? Are we equipping believers to influence culture? Are we more focused on getting the world to come to us rather than using our resources to go out into the world? These are challenging but necessary questions for every church and believer to reflect on.

The original system Jesus designed for the church includes essential features foundational to its mission. We've already discussed Kingdom authority, including the power Jesus gave His followers to bind and loose. Discipleship and baptism, however, are more than tasks to complete—they are central to the church's purpose. Jesus called us to make disciples of all nations, not merely to seek conversions but to immerse people in His teachings and equip them to become transformational agents in the world.

Another key feature is strategic engagement. For the church to bring about true transformation, it must engage with every sphere of society—political, economic, cultural, and spiritual. This might look like advocating for just policies in government, empowering the poor by providing tools and resources for financial success, shaping arts and entertainment by creating content that reflects biblical truths and promotes moral integrity, and providing spiritual leadership through discipleship and prayer in the community. Each of these areas presents opportunities for the church to bring Kingdom values to bear and make a lasting impact. Strategic engagement is not an option; it is vital to the church's role as the Ekklesia.

Spiritual engagement is also crucial. The church is called to recognize and confront spiritual strongholds that stand in the way of advancing God's Kingdom. Through prayer, fasting, and the use of the gifts of the Holy Spirit, believers are equipped to dismantle these strongholds and bring freedom to individuals and communities. The battle is physical and spiritual; the church must be equipped to fight in both realms.

Lastly, the church must prioritize community and collaboration. Jesus never intended for His followers to accomplish the mission alone. The early church thrived because it was a unified community, sharing resources, supporting one another, and working together toward a common goal. Today's church must rediscover this spirit of unity and collaboration, recognizing that we are stronger together and that the mission of discipling nations requires the collective effort of the entire body of Christ.

These features—Kingdom authority, strategic and spiritual engagement, discipleship, and community—are not optional. They are integral to what it means to be the Ekklesia. Reinstalling the original system that Jesus designed requires intentional effort, a willingness to embrace change, and a realignment with the church's true identity and purpose. But the rewards are transformative. By returning to the design Jesus laid out, we become fully a part of what He is building and can again become the world-changing force we were meant to be. This is the path to discipling nations, advancing the Kingdom of God, and ultimately, changing the course of history for His glory.

New Evaluation Methods

As we reinstall EkklesiaOS, it is crucial to establish new success measurements. While traditional metrics, such as buildings, bodies, and budgets are important, they are not the ultimate indicators of a healthy Ekklesia. Instead, we must evaluate our success based on our local, regional, and global impact.

One key measurement should be the level of transformation in the communities and nations where the Ekklesia is present. This includes social, economic, and spiritual changes that align with the values of the Kingdom of God. Are we seeing justice where there was injustice? Are families being restored? Is there a decrease in crime and corruption? These are some of the indicators that the Ekklesia is fulfilling its mission.

We must also develop tools and methods beyond traditional church metrics to measure transformation effectively. For example, crime statistics and economic indicators can provide tangible evidence of the impact of the Ekklesia. Testimonies of changed lives; people moving in signs, wonders, and miracles; restored relationships; and renewed hope are powerful indicators of spiritual transformation.

Another critical measurement is the depth and breadth of discipleship. Are we merely making converts, or are we truly discipling people to live out the Word of God in the power of the Holy Spirit in every aspect of their lives? This involves not just knowledge but transformation—seeing individuals grow in their faith, character, and ability to influence others for the Kingdom. The multiplication of disciples should also be a measure of discipleship. Are those we disciple going on to disciple others? This exponential growth indicates that the Ekklesia is functioning as intended, spreading the Gospel and Kingdom values into the fabric of everyday life.

Finally, we should measure our engagement in the seven spheres of society: government, education, business, media, arts/entertainment, family, and the church. The true impact of the Ekklesia is not confined to the walls of the church but is seen when believers take their faith public, actively influencing the world around them. Are believers bringing their Christian values into the workplace, the political arena, the arts, and other areas where culture is shaped? The effectiveness of the Ekklesia can be measured by how much it impacts and transforms these societal spheres, advancing God's Kingdom in tangible ways.

To measure this community engagement, we might begin by identifying how many believers are involved in public service, in leadership positions, or in spearheading cultural initiatives. Are Christians taking on roles as elected officials, educators, business leaders, or artists where they can shape policies, values, and culture? Tracking this can provide a clear picture of how faith is integrated into broader societal functions. Additionally, we can assess the influence of Christian values by examining trends in public opinion, education curricula, business ethics, and media content. For example, are businesses implementing ethical guidelines that reflect biblical principles? Are media outlets and artistic projects showing a positive shift toward values like integrity, justice, and purity? By evaluating these trends, we can gain insight into how effectively believers are influencing the culture around them.

This type of measurement requires patience and a long-term perspective. Cultural transformation does not happen overnight but through a gradual process of believers consistently living out their faith in their daily interactions and professional roles. As we engage more intentionally in these spheres, we can expect gradual but meaningful changes in the societal landscape over time, one person at a time.

Unleash the Army

The final step in restoring the church as the Ekklesia is to unleash an army of believers who are equipped, empowered, and ready to take on the challenges of transforming their neighborhoods and nations. This involves training, equipping, and mobilizing the Ekklesia to operate effectively in their God-given authority. An essential part of this is providing vision to all believers, including leaders, helping them understand the bigger mission and how their unique gifts, callings, and influence are vital in advancing God's Kingdom throughout every corner of public and private life.

The first step in unleashing this army is comprehensive training. Believers must be equipped with a deep understanding of their full identity in Christ, the authority they carry, and the mission they are called to fulfill. This training should be practical, focusing on how to apply biblical principles in real-world situations.

Training should include teaching on Sonship, intercession and the gifts of the Spirit, as well as practical skills like leadership, communication, and strategic planning. Providing ongoing mentorship and support is essential to help believers grow in their calling and overcome challenges. In addition to formal training programs, churches can create opportunities for experiential learning. Mission trips, community service projects, and evangelism outreaches allow believers to put their training into practice and gain confidence in their ability to influence the world for Christ.

Once equipped, believers must be mobilized to act. This involves creating opportunities for engagement, whether through community projects, political activism, or school system involvement.

The Ekklesia should be a dynamic force, constantly moving forward to bring about the Kingdom of God on Earth. This mobilization also requires leadership. The Ekklesia needs strong, visionary pastors and leaders who can guide and inspire others to step out in faith and take bold action. These pastors and leaders should be servant-hearted and focused on empowering others rather than building their platforms.

To effectively mobilize the Ekklesia, churches should develop clear strategies and goals. This might include identifying critical areas shaping culture that need transformation, organizing teams to address specific issues, and providing resources to support these efforts. Communication is also crucial; believers must be informed and inspired about the mission and how to participate.

Finally, sustaining the movement requires ongoing support and encouragement. The Ekklesia must be a community that exhorts, nurtures and supports its members, providing the resources and relationships needed to persevere in the mission. This includes accountability, prayer support, and practical help.

As the Ekklesia grows and expands its influence, it is crucial to focus on the mission. This means continually evaluating our strategies and methods and adjusting to align with God's purposes. It also means celebrating big and small victories as evidence of God's Kingdom advancing on Earth.

Sustaining the movement also involves creating a culture of empowerment within the church. This means encouraging innovation, allowing for mistakes and learning opportunities, and recognizing and developing the gifts and callings of all believers. When people feel valued and supported, they are more likely to stay engaged and committed to the mission.

An Awakened Identity

Imagine Aragorn from *The Lord of the Rings*, living for years as a ranger, a protector in the shadows, knowing his true destiny yet fearful to step into it. Though he fought valiantly and with honor, it wasn't until he finally embraced his full identity as the rightful king of Gondor that his purpose and authority truly came alive. His awakening to who he truly was changed everything—not just for him but for everyone he was called to lead. With this step of faith, Aragorn emerged out of obscurity and into the calling that awaited him, rising with new confidence, authority, and purpose. This is the power of an *awakened identity*.

Similarly, as explored in the previous sections, our relational identity as sons and daughters is foundational to our functional identity as the Ekklesia. We are His children, called to do His work on Earth, representing His Kingdom and carrying His authority wherever we go. The revelation that God is our Father and we are His sons and daughters gives us the confidence and authority to partner with Jesus in building His Ekklesia. This relational foundation empowers us to operate from a place of love, security, and co-laboring with Christ, free from fear or striving.

With this understanding of our full identity—relationally as sons and daughters, and functionally as the Ekklesia—we are now positioned to live with an *awakened identity*. This means living fully aware of who we are in Christ and of the authority we carry to influence and transform the world around us. It calls us to step beyond the walls of the church building and engage with the world as Jesus and the early Ekklesia did. The world awaits the manifestation of the sons and daughters of God, and as the Ekklesia, we are commissioned to bring the fullness of the Kingdom to every sphere of society.

In the next section, we will explore what it means to live with this awakened identity. Like Aragorn, who embraced his calling as king, or Gideon, who discovered he was a warrior chosen to lead Israel with God's strength, this awakening empowered them to move beyond their fears and limitations, fully engaging in their purpose and transforming their world. In the same way, our own awakened identity as sons and daughters frees us to step beyond the church walls and into a life of influence, bringing transformation and advancing the Kingdom of God in every sphere.

SECTION 3

Change the World

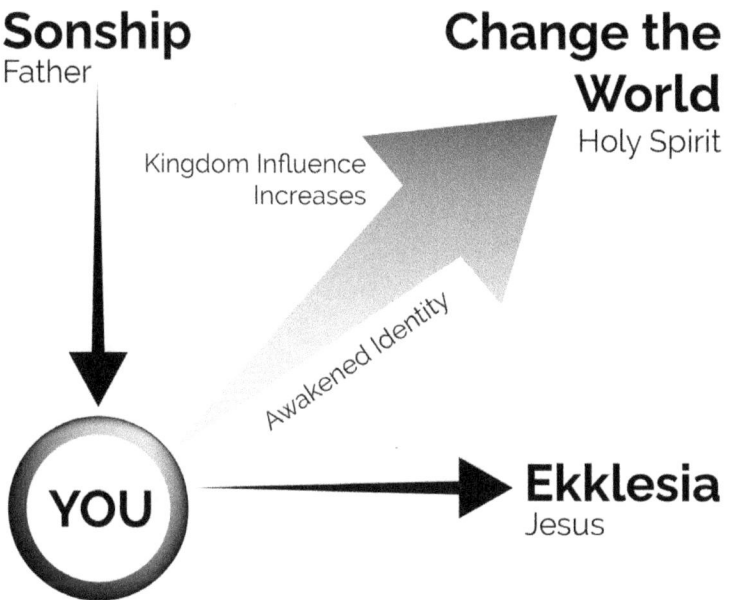

8.
The Convergence of Sonship and Ekklesia

It took me more than 40 years of walking with the Lord and over 30 years in full-time ministry before I finally grasped the fullness of stewarding my identity in Christ through Sonship and Ekklesia. Looking back, I sometimes wonder why it took so long. I've even questioned whether all the years prior—my walk with the Lord and my ministry assignment—had been in vain. Thankfully, the answer is no, not at all. We have seen countless lives transformed, and the fruit of our ministry has been abundant. Every step of the journey regarding my identity mattered. Those years were never wasted; they were all part of the process. And the lives changed through our walk with the Lord stand as a testament to His faithfulness.

Yet, as I reflect on that journey, I now see there was something I hadn't fully realized. Though my love for God was genuine and my ministry sincere, I found myself living from an orphan mindset. Because of this, I had an incomplete vision of who I was to the Father and my role in His Kingdom. I wasn't just called to work for God—I was called to live from Him and partner with Jesus in building His Ekklesia. Until I embraced this reality, I was functioning from a limitation rather than the fullness of my identity in Him.

When the revelation of these greater realities finally broke through, it was as if everything suddenly fell into place. My life and ministry, came together with clarity and purpose. I realized that God was calling me to work, live and minister from a place of intimacy with Him as His son. I no longer need to strive or compete as I once did. I'm not driven by the pressure to prove myself, nor am I caught up in the comparison game that often characterizes ministry. Instead, I've entered a new season—one marked by rest, peace, and confidence, grounded in the knowledge that I am His son, and I am operating *from* that identity, not *for* it.

Moreover, my understanding of the church and its mission has become crystal clear. I now see that the church is not simply a gathering of believers but the Ekklesia—Christ's governing assembly on Earth, commissioned to bring Heaven's influence into the world around us. The measurement for "church" success is not the pressure to increase attendance, but the extent to which the Kingdom influences and shapes lives, families, and culture. For the first time, it feels entirely right—because it is right. I no longer have an incomplete understanding, which has changed everything. Now, life and ministry flow from a place of security in who I am and what I am called to do, and the results are no longer the fruit of striving but of resting in Him.

My identity is *awakened*.

This awakening to who we are in God is an unfolding revelation. From the moment we encounter Christ, we begin to awaken to a new identity that transforms every aspect of our lives. This transformation starts with understanding ourselves as sons and daughters of a good Heavenly Father. But it does not end there.

Our *awakened identity* also calls us to participate in a mission beyond ourselves—an identity rooted in our function as Christ's Ekklesia, His governing body on Earth. Our identity in Sonship and Ekklesia, is inseparably woven together, forming one awakened identity through which we live from the love of the Father and the authority of his Kingdom.

In the previous chapters, we explored the richness of Sonship. Like Jesus, we saw that to be a son or daughter of God is to live from a place of deep intimacy with the Father. It's an identity that isn't earned by works but received by grace. Sonship is the foundation of everything we do; it's the source of our security, confidence, and sense of purpose. We are loved simply because we are His.

On the other hand, the chapters on Ekklesia emphasized the unique commission given to us as sons and daughters. Ekklesia is the call to govern, legislate, and bring Heaven to Earth. As Christ's Ekklesia, we are more than a gathering of believers; we are His ambassadors, called to exercise His authority in every sphere of life. But here is where the two converge: Our authority as the Ekklesia is rooted in our intimacy as sons and daughters. In other words, the revelation of Sonship fuels the function of Ekklesia. Without the love of the Father, the power of the Ekklesia is incomplete. Without the commission of the Ekklesia, the relationship of Sonship remains dormant.

Sonship is the foundation of our identity in Christ, revealing God as Abba, our loving Father, and shaping our relationship with Him. From the beginning, God intended for us to live in intimate fellowship with Him, as seen in Adam and Eve's perfect connection before the Fall. Romans 8:15 captures this beautifully: "The Spirit you received brought about your adoption to Sonship. And by Him, we cry, 'Abba, Father.'" This cry speaks to our belonging and deep-rooted connection to the One who created us. No longer orphans, we are free from fear and the need for performance-based validation, knowing our value comes from being God's children. This deep assurance allows us to walk in freedom, secure and significant in Christ, regardless of our circumstances.

However, Sonship doesn't stop at personal intimacy; it propels us outward, compelling us to partner with God in His mission for the world. The love we receive from the Father is not meant to be hoarded but shared. The Ekklesia comes in here—our collective identity and mission to bring God's Kingdom to the world. As His children, we are called to be His representatives, carrying the love and authority of Sonship into every sphere of society, advancing His purposes, and transforming the world.

Thus, an *awakened identity* is the convergence of both Sonship and Ekklesia, where we are both fully loved and commissioned.

The Perfect Example

Jesus is the perfect example of what it means to live fully as both Son and Ekklesia. Throughout His earthly ministry, Jesus demonstrated how intimacy with the Father and the authority of the Kingdom work hand in hand. He never separated His identity as the Son from His mission to bring Heaven to Earth. Instead, He lived in the perfect convergence of Sonship and Ekklesia, showing us what is possible when we embrace both aspects of our awakened identity.

Jesus's life was a constant expression of Sonship. He repeatedly referred to God as "Father" and lived in continual communion with Him. In John 5:19, Jesus said, "The Son can do nothing by Himself; He can do only what He sees His Father doing because whatever the Father does, the Son also does." This statement reveals the depth of Jesus's intimacy with His Father. His every action flowed from His relationship with the Father in the power of the Holy Spirit. He knew He was fully loved, accepted, and secure in that love. Jesus modeled what it looks like to live from the Father's embrace, never striving for approval, never *reacting* to the devil, but always, *responding* to the Father, ministering from a place of deep connection.

Yet, Jesus also embodied the authority of the Ekklesia. As the Son, He carried out His Father's will with power and authority. One of the clearest demonstrations of this was when He declared, "Your Kingdom come, Your will be done, on Earth as it is in Heaven" (Matthew 6:10). This was not just a prayer; it was Jesus's mandate. As Son, everywhere Jesus went, He brought the Kingdom of Heaven into earthly reality. Whether it was healing the sick, casting out demons, or confronting injustice, Jesus ministered with the authority that the Father had given Him. He did not simply love the Father; He governed on His behalf, revealing what it means to exercise Kingdom authority.

We see this in Jesus's healing ministry. In Matthew 8, a Roman centurion came to Jesus, asking Him to heal his servant, who was paralyzed and in terrible suffering. Jesus responded immediately, saying, "I will go and heal him" (Matthew 8:7). But the centurion's faith amazed Jesus, as he acknowledged Jesus's authority over sickness, saying, "Just say the word, and my servant will be healed" (Matthew 8:8). Jesus marveled at his faith and, from a distance, spoke healing over the servant, who was instantly made well.

This act of healing was not just a miracle; it was, in fact, a demonstration of the power and authority Jesus carried as the Son and the Ekklesia. He did not need to perform elaborate rituals or prayers. He spoke the word because He knew His authority came from His relationship with the Father.

He understood that as the Son, He had the authority to release healing, and as the Ekklesia, He had the responsibility to bring the Kingdom's power into that situation. Jesus modeled the convergence of Sonship and Ekklesia, showing us that healing is not something we have to strive for but something we can release through the anointing of the Holy Spirit.

Jesus is our example of what's possible when we live in the fullness of our *awakened identity*. He showed us that Sonship and Ekklesia are not meant to be separate realities. Instead, they are two expressions of the same Kingdom life. We are invited into the same relationship with the Father that Jesus enjoyed and given the same authority to bring Heaven to Earth.

As followers of Christ, we are called to live as Jesus did—to be secure in our identity as sons and daughters and empowered to govern as His Ekklesia. Jesus demonstrated what is possible when we live from the Father's love and carry out His mission with authority. Healing the sick, releasing freedom to the oppressed, and bringing God's will to Earth are not exclusive to Jesus—they are part of our calling, too. He is our model, and through Him, we see that this life of intimacy and power is available to us. The question is, will we step into the fullness of our *awakened identity* as Jesus demonstrated?

The Apostle Paul

The Apostle Paul is another powerful example of someone who lived fully in his *awakened identity* both in Sonship and as a representative of Christ's Ekklesia. Throughout his ministry, Paul demonstrated how intimacy with the Father and Kingdom authority could be lived out practically and powerfully. His life and letters reflect his understanding of Sonship, as he often wrote about being adopted into God's family and living as a child of God. Simultaneously, Paul walked in the authority of the Ekklesia, performing signs and wonders that transformed communities and advanced the Kingdom of God.

Paul's understanding of Sonship is evident through his profound relationship with God as Father. He often spoke of the believer's adoption as sons and daughters of God, emphasizing that we are no longer slaves but heirs with Christ.

For Paul, Sonship was foundational to his identity in Christ. It gave him the assurance and confidence to minister without fear or striving, serving from God's approval, not for it. He knew he was fully accepted and loved by the Father, and this revelation of Sonship fueled his ministry.

Paul's understanding of Sonship went beyond mere intimacy with the Father; through this identity, as the Holy Spirit worked within him, he found the passion and purpose to live out Christ's Ekklesia. This empowered him to walk in the authority of the Ekklesia, representing Christ and demonstrating Kingdom power wherever he went.

Paul's ministry was consistently marked by miracles and supernatural signs, bearing witness to the power of the Gospel. One of the most remarkable examples of Paul functioning as the Ekklesia is found in Acts 19, where Luke records that "God did extraordinary miracles through Paul" (Acts 19:11). In this passage, Paul was in Ephesus, ministering to a city steeped in idolatry and spiritual darkness. During his time there, the power of the Holy Spirit flowed so strongly through him that even handkerchiefs and aprons that touched Paul were taken to the sick, their illnesses were cured, and evil spirits left them (Acts 19:12).

This was not a typical healing ministry—these were extraordinary miracles, displaying the authority Paul carried as a son within Christ's Ekklesia. The impact of these miracles was so profound that many people in the city turned from their sorcery and burned their scrolls publicly in repentance, leading to a massive revival in the region (Acts 19:18-19).

Paul's ability to walk in such extraordinary power did not come from his own strength or skill. It was rooted in his relationship with the Father, in Christ. Paul knew that as a son, he had access to the authority of Heaven. He lived in the reality of Sonship, which gave him the confidence to release the supernatural power of God wherever he went. As part of the Ekklesia, Paul recognized that he had been given authority to bring the Kingdom of God into the darkest places and to see people set free, healed, and transformed.

Paul's life is a powerful demonstration of the convergence of Sonship and Ekklesia. He lived in communion with the Father, based on the finished work of Christ, fully aware of his identity as a son. But he also understood that this identity came with a responsibility to carry out the mission of the Kingdom out of the overflow of His relationship with His Father. As the Ekklesia, Paul walked in authority, performing miracles and transforming communities through the power of The Holy Spirit. His life shows us that Sonship and Ekklesia are not separate aspects of our identity but two sides of the same coin. One empowers the other; intimacy with the Father fuels our authority to bring His Kingdom to Earth.

Paul exemplifies what is possible when we live in the fullness of our *awakened identity*. He shows us that we can experience the Father's love while walking in the authority of the Ekklesia. Like Paul, we are called to live as sons and daughters fully loved and accepted by the Father. But we are also called to exercise the authority of Christ, bringing His healing, freedom, and transformation to the world around us.

Through Paul's example, we see that extraordinary miracles and Kingdom impact are possible when we live from the fullness of our identity in Christ. The question remains: Will we, like Jesus and Paul, step into the fullness of our Sonship and live as the Ekklesia, bringing the reality of Heaven to Earth?

Framework of Awakened Identity

The convergence of Sonship and Ekklesia brings us to the heart of our *awakened identity*. To live as sons and daughters of God is to carry His heart wherever we go, and to live as the Ekklesia is to establish His Kingdom in every place we step. Together, they empower us to live fully, both relationally and functionally.

This awakened identity carries distinct expressions, each revealing a vital aspect of how we live, lead, and impact the world. Let's explore these key distinctions and how they shape our lives.

Focus

An awakened identity provides focus by giving us clarity of purpose and direction in how we live and lead. Without understanding who we are in Christ, we can become scattered, pulled in different directions, striving for meaning, or reacting to life's demands rather than moving with intentionality. But when we embrace our *awakened identity*, we are no longer guessing at our purpose; we live with focus because we know who we are and what we are called to do.

This focus is both *relational and functional*, rooted in intimacy with the Father and expressed through Kingdom impact. *Sonship* secures us in the Father's love, while *Ekklesia* commissions us to bring Heaven's culture into the world. Together, they provide the focus needed for a fruitful life—one that is deeply rooted in His love and actively engaged in His mission.

Authority

The authority we receive through Sonship and Ekklesia is not just a concept—it is the foundation for how we live, lead, and advance God's Kingdom. As sons and daughters, our authority is not earned but inherited, flowing from intimacy with the Father and empowering us to govern according to His heart. *Sonship secures our identity; Ekklesia commissions our assignment.*

Jesus entrusts His Ekklesia with *functional authority*, giving us the keys of the Kingdom to bind and loose, to establish Heaven's will on Earth, and to push back the Gates of Hades. But authority is only effective when it is *rooted in Sonship*. Without intimacy with the Father, authority becomes a title without power, and action turns into striving rather than Spirit-led impact. When we embrace our awakened identity, we move with confidence—governing from love, leading from security, and advancing His Kingdom with Heaven's backing.

Prayer

In our awakened identity, prayer is where Sonship and Ekklesia converge, creating a powerful synergy between intimacy and authority. As sons and daughters, prayer is not just a practice—it is communion with the Father, a place where we rest in His presence, hear His voice, and grow in our relationship with Him. But as the Ekklesia, prayer is also our means of governing with Him—declaring His will, interceding for the world, and advancing His Kingdom on Earth.

We do not pray as beggars hoping for change, but as *heirs partnering with God to establish His purposes*. Our prayers carry weight because they flow from the authority we've received as Ekklesia, rooted in the intimacy we experience through Sonship. When we embrace this reality, our prayers shift from passive petitions to bold, Kingdom-decrees that shape history and impact nations.

Solutions

When we walk in our awakened identity—Sonship and Ekklesia—wisdom becomes available to us in a way the world cannot comprehend. As sons and daughters, we are connected to the Father, receiving His heart and perspective. As His Ekklesia, we are entrusted with His authority to bring Heaven's solutions into the Earth. Wisdom is the bridge between the two, equipping us to discern, create, and implement answers the world is desperately searching for.

This kind of wisdom is not just knowledge—it is divine strategy. It empowers us to step into real world challenges with godly insight that reflect Heaven's design. *We don't just see problems; we bring solutions*. Wisdom is how we live out our awakened identity—turning revelation into action and solutions that transform the world.

Impact

Imagine a people who live fully awakened to their identity as sons and daughters of God—secure in His love, walking in the freedom and confidence of their inheritance. No longer striving for approval or bound by fear, they reflect the Father's heart in everything they do. Their lives overflow with His love, shaping their relationships, decisions, and the way they influence the world around them.

Now, picture a world transformed by these awakened sons and daughters. Governments would operate with righteousness and justice, businesses would thrive on integrity and generosity, and schools would shape minds with God's wisdom and truth.

Not only would governing systems be renewed, but media would also proclaim what is good and honorable, arts and entertainment would reflect purity and creativity, and families would flourish on strong, godly foundations. Faith would no longer be confined to church buildings but would actively transform culture, influence policy, shape industry, and restore community.

When we as sons and daughters step fully into our calling as the Ekklesia, our influence extends beyond personal transformation into societal reformation. Together, we create a movement that shifts nations toward God's original intent. This is the impact of a fully awakened identity—where Sonship fuels the heart and Ekklesia carries out the mission, working as one to bring the reality of Heaven to Earth.

Moving Forward in Awakened Identity

As we continue to discover what living from our awakened identity means, we must hold fast to the convergence of Sonship and Ekklesia. Our identity is relational and functional, and it is only in integrating the two that we step into the fullness of what God has called us to be.

Our lives are rooted in the Father's love, and from that love, we are empowered to bring His Kingdom to Earth. We are called to live close to the Father's heart through Christ, experiencing His love and intimacy daily. We also have the privilege of co-laboring with Jesus to carry out His mission, bringing Heaven's culture into every area of life. This is the essence of true Christianity, an *awakened identity*—fully loved, fully empowered, and fully alive in Christ.

Moving forward, we will explore how this identity manifests in everyday life, from personal relationships to cultural influence. We will see how the revelation of Sonship and the authority of Ekklesia shape every aspect of who we are and what we do, empowering us to change the world for God's glory.

This is our *awakened identity*—and it changes everything.

9.
Beyond the Walls

A few years ago, our church hosted a two-day event in the heart of Silicon Valley, similar to TED Talks but focused on Christ-centered tech entrepreneurs—individuals using their creativity in the tech world to advance the Kingdom of God.

We gathered at Google headquarters on Friday, with the event shifting to our church on Saturday. I was eager to see these innovative followers of Jesus using their unique gifts in technology to serve God's purposes. Like in TED Talks, presenters had 20 minutes to showcase their work.

Before the Saturday session started, the event's creator approached me with a special request. She asked if I could introduce myself as the Senior Pastor, welcome everyone, and validate them and their work as genuine ministry. I gladly agreed but couldn't help asking why she felt I needed to validate their work. She explained that many participants felt their churches only recognized or valued ministry within the church walls and that their contributions in the marketplace—their innovations and careers—were often dismissed as non-ministry.

I was stunned to hear that. It was clear how important it was for me, as a senior pastor, to affirm these men and women—to help them see that they are called as ministers beyond the church walls, and that their passion, talents, and work outside the church was just as much ministry as serving in ministry within the church.

Standing before them that day, I expressed my gratitude for their gifts and calling. I thanked them for their commitment to advancing God's Kingdom in ways that reach into places the traditional church cannot. I reminded them that their work is worship to the Lord and within their fields of work they were salt, light, and leaven—releasing the wisdom of God through their creativity to change the world.

Reflecting on that moment affirmed how much we've limited our understanding of ministry to what happens within the church. Yet, God's Kingdom operates beyond those walls—in the everyday places, the small yet powerful ways we influence the world around us.

The Small and the Miraculous

I've discovered the Kingdom of God advances in two profound ways: through the power of the small and the power of the miraculous. Both are essential to fulfilling our mission to bring transformation to the world. The power of the small represents the quiet, subtle influence of our everyday actions, often unnoticed but undeniably transformative over time. At the same time, the power of the miraculous showcases God's ability to step into the natural world and do the impossible, revealing His supernatural authority and love.

The world understands the power of the small. It often uses subtle, seemingly insignificant moments to gain entrance and influence in our lives, gradually shaping our beliefs, values, and behaviors without drawing immediate attention. These small, intentional acts are strategically placed to create a lasting impression, slowly permeating our culture. Whether through media, advertising, or everyday interactions, small, deliberate actions are often the gateway for broader cultural shifts.

Take, for instance, a subtle yet deliberate moment in modern culture. In *Star Wars: The Force Awakens*, Disney inserted a brief, two-second clip of two women kissing. Though this scene is contrary to biblical truth and sparked some controversy, the intent was to shape cultural perception. Disney understood that even the smallest moments can influence culture, subtly embedding a narrative without fanfare. These subtle moments may not cause an immediate stir, but over time, they accumulate, shaping thoughts, redefining norms, and influencing values. This is the power of the small: small, deliberate actions that work like seeds planted in fertile soil, growing slowly but steadily into something much larger.

However, while the power of the small is significant, it is not the whole picture. The small and the miraculous are constantly in play; together, they drive true Kingdom transformation. The world can adopt the power of the small and leverage it to shift cultures and norms. Still, it cannot replicate the power of the miraculous—those moments when God steps into the natural world and does what is beyond human capability.

The two must be pursued together. Subtle influence and miraculous intervention are not separate forces but complementary elements of the Kingdom of God. As believers, we are called to engage in both as we recognize that the small can shape hearts while the miraculous reveals God's nature and power instantly.

Throughout history, we've seen miracles that defy human understanding—people being healed of terminal diseases like cancer, creative miracles where limbs are restored, eyesight is given to the blind, or the dead are brought back to life. These are not mere stories from ancient times but realities that still occur today, demonstrating God's ability to intervene directly in our lives. The power of the miraculous showcases God's authority over the perceived impossibilities, demonstrating His love for humanity and His desire to bring healing and restoration.

The beautiful thing about God's Kingdom is that He invites us to minister in both ways. As sons and daughters of Christ's Ekklesia, we are called to participate in both the small and the miraculous. Through the power of the Holy Spirit, we are equipped to engage in the subtle, everyday moments that transform society while also being vessels for God's miraculous power to break into the natural world. We don't need to choose between the two; we can operate in both.

Power of the Small

Jesus often illustrated the power of the small in His teachings on the Kingdom of God. He used metaphors like salt, light, and leaven to show how small, faithful actions have a far-reaching impact.

Salt: Preserving and Enhancing the World

In Matthew 5:13, Jesus said, "You are the salt of the Earth." Salt is a small substance, but its influence is substantial. In ancient times, salt was primarily used as a preservative. It was rubbed into meat to slow decay, symbolizing how we, as believers, are called to preserve righteousness and truth in a world that naturally leans toward moral decay. Our role may seem small—standing for integrity in the workplace, showing kindness to a neighbor, or being patient in difficult circumstances—but these actions prevent our communities from spiraling into chaos and upholding what is biblically good and true. We are like salt, subtly preserving the world from moral decay.

Salt also enhances flavor. Just as a pinch of salt makes food more enjoyable, we are called to bring God's love and truth into our environments, making them richer and more meaningful. Think of Joseph in Egypt, Daniel in Babylon, and Esther in Persia. They lived in ungodly cultures, but their presence flavored their surroundings with God's wisdom, hope, and favor. Their small, faithful actions didn't immediately change their environments, but their influence transformed them over time.

Salt's power lies not in its visibility but in its effect. You don't often notice the salt on your food, but you certainly notice when it's missing. In the same way, our small acts of faith, even when unnoticed, can have a preserving and enhancing effect on the world. This is the power of the small, faithfully living each day in a way that reflects God's truth and brings His goodness into the world.

Light: Shining in the Darkness

Jesus also said, "You are the light of the world" (Matthew 5:14). Though small, light can effortlessly overcome darkness. Even a tiny candle can illuminate an entire room. In a world filled with confusion, fear, and spiritual blindness, our lives are meant to shine, providing hope, clarity, and direction to those around us.

Light doesn't need to force its way into darkness; it simply shines. Likewise, we can influence the world without a *huge anointing* or extraordinary gifts. We shine brightly by living biblically, with integrity, showing love, and reflecting Christ in everyday interactions. Jesus calls us to let our light shine before others so they may see our good works and glorify our Father in Heaven. The power of light is that it enables others to see more clearly. Our actions, however small, can help people see the truth of who God is and the reality of His Kingdom.

The world is full of darkness—brokenness, fear, and confusion—but even small acts of light can pierce through overwhelming darkness. When we show kindness, serve others, or offer a word of encouragement in His name, we are lighting the way for others to encounter the love and truth of God. These seemingly small actions, when done consistently, light up the world around us and help others see who Christ is. These actions create pathways into the hearts of others, preparing them to hear and receive the life-changing message of the gospel.

Leaven: Transforming Culture from Within

In Matthew 13:33, Jesus compares the Kingdom of God to leaven. When leaven (yeast), though small, is mixed into the dough and activated, it spreads and causes the entire loaf to rise. This compelling picture shows how small, faithful actions in God's Kingdom, activated by the Holy Spirit, can transform society from within.

Leaven doesn't work by remaining outside the dough—it must be worked into it and mixed thoroughly before it begins to change the entire batch. But the leaven of God's Kingdom is no ordinary leaven; it is supernatural. Like natural leaven, nothing can stop its effect once it is introduced and worked into the dough. It quietly and relentlessly permeates the entire lump, transforming it from within. But Kingdom leaven goes even further—it carries supernatural ingredients designed to bring deep and lasting change.

Once Kingdom leaven is sown into culture, it becomes unstoppable. It doesn't rely on human effort or manipulation; the leaven's power to transform is inherent. All that is required is for the Ekklesia—the church called to govern and influence culture—to sow the leaven. Once sown, this supernatural leaven is activated by the Holy Spirit, influences and changes everything it touches. It spreads quietly yet powerfully and carries the ability to bring about radical transformation. The leaven itself holds the power to create change, working invisibly yet undeniably, much like the Kingdom of God working through the faithful actions of believers.

As sons and daughters, we are called to be like leaven in the world. We are not meant to isolate ourselves within the four walls of the church but to be activated, worked into the fabric of society, quietly and steadily bringing about transformation in the power of the Holy Spirit. Whether in business, education, government, or the arts, we can influence culture from within by carrying the presence of God into every sphere of life.

Consider someone who consistently demonstrates kindness and integrity in the workplace. While others may cut corners or prioritize self-interest, this individual chooses to do the right thing and offers help, encouragement, and respect to everyone, regardless of rank or status. Over time, their consistent behavior begins to leaven the office atmosphere. Colleagues start to emulate their example, trust grows, and a healthier, more Kingdom-valued work environment emerges. This is the subtle power of leaven—small actions quietly working to transform the larger culture.

In neighborhoods, small acts of service can also function as leaven. A family that regularly offers help to their neighbors—bringing meals to someone in need, offering to babysit, or simply being available to listen—can slowly create a sense of community and trust. Their quiet acts of kindness inspire others to do the same, leading to a neighborhood culture of mutual support and care. It may start with one family, but over time, it spreads, influencing the entire community. This is how leaven works—small, faithful actions that grow into something much larger, impacting lives in ways that extend beyond the initial effort.

The power of leaven is its subtlety. Just a small amount of leaven can transform an entire loaf of bread. Likewise, our small acts of kindness—whether through serving, loving, or speaking the truth in love—have the power to permeate and transform the culture around us. We may not see immediate results, but these small, faithful actions have a profound impact over time, influencing society for God's Kingdom.

Power of the Miraculous

While the power of the small is essential for advancing the Kingdom of God, another dynamic cannot be ignored: the power of the miraculous. Miracles, signs, and wonders are supernatural interventions that reveal God's nature and demonstrate His authority over creation. These events are powerful testimonies of God's love, compassion, and desire to restore and heal. While the small acts of faithfulness quietly permeate and influence culture, the miraculous breaks into the natural world in undeniable ways, demonstrating God's ability to do what seems impossible. As believers, we are called to walk in both areas—the small, everyday acts of serving others and the supernatural expressions of God's Kingdom.

Miracles, signs, and wonders are not simply isolated events from biblical history; they are part of the ongoing work of the Holy Spirit in the world today. God still heals the sick, performs creative miracles, and demonstrates His power in ways that draw people to Him. These miraculous moments often open the door for more profound transformation, both in the lives of those who experience them and in the hearts of those who witness them. Let's explore how God uses miracles, signs, and wonders to reveal His Kingdom and invite us into a greater understanding of His nature.

Miracles: Demonstrating God's Supernatural Power

Miracles are extraordinary acts of God's power that defy natural explanation. They are God's supernatural intervention in human situations that demonstrate His authority over sickness, disease, death, and natural elements. Miracles often involve dramatic healings, such as when people are cured of terminal illnesses like cancer or when the blind receive their sight. They are not random occurrences but specific acts of God that reveal His ability to bring life where there was none.

For example, in the New Testament, we read about Jesus healing people who were paralyzed for years and restoring them to full health. In modern times, we hear testimonies of people who were diagnosed with terminal cancer, only to be completely healed by the Lord, even after doctors had given up hope. These miracles remind us that the constraints of the natural world do not limit God. He can and does intervene in ways that defy medical understanding and human logic.

But miracles are not just about healing the body; they can also involve supernatural provision, as in the case of Jesus feeding the five thousand with just five loaves and two fish (John 6:1-14). This miracle wasn't simply about feeding a crowd—it reveals the heart of the Father as a provider who cares deeply about the needs of His people. God continues to work this way today, providing for His children miraculously, often when all other resources seem exhausted.

Signs: Pointing to a Greater Reality

Signs are supernatural acts that point beyond themselves to a greater reality. They are visible evidence of God's power and presence, directing people's attention to His Kingdom. While a sign may be miraculous, its primary purpose is to reveal something greater about God's nature and intentions.

In the New Testament, signs often accompanied the preaching of the Gospel, confirming the truth of the message. For instance, when Jesus healed the sick and cast out demons, these acts were signs pointing to the arrival of God's Kingdom on Earth. The people witnessing these signs recognized that they were encountering something greater than just physical healing—they were seeing the power of God made manifest in their midst.

Signs also reveal the authority of Jesus and the work of the Holy Spirit in believers. Jesus promised in Mark 16:17-18 that signs would follow those who believe in Him: "In My name they will cast out demons; they will speak with new tongues … they will lay hands on the sick, and they will recover." These signs point to the reality that God is at work through His people, confirming the message of salvation and the ongoing presence of His Kingdom.

Today, signs continue to accompany the work of the Holy Spirit. When we see miraculous healings, deliverance from oppression, or supernatural protection, these signs point to God's active presence in our world. They reveal that the Kingdom of God is advancing, not just in spiritual or abstract ways, but in tangible, visible acts of power.

Wonders: Revealing the Majesty of God

Wonders are supernatural events that leave people in awe, revealing God's majesty and glory. While signs point to a greater reality, wonders captivate the hearts and minds of those who witness them and often lead to a sense of reverence and amazement at God's power. Wonders are frequently mentioned alongside signs in Scripture, and together, they serve to demonstrate the grandeur of God's Kingdom breaking into the natural world.

Wonders often defy human explanation, leaving no doubt that God has intervened. In the Book of Acts, we see numerous wonders that astonished both believers and unbelievers alike—such as tongues of fire appearing at Pentecost (Acts 2:3), Peter's shadow healing the sick, Philip being supernaturally transported after baptizing the Ethiopian eunuch, and an earthquake opening prison doors and breaking chains. These wonders were not just displays of power; they were divine invitations for people to encounter the living God in a deeply personal and transformative way.

The miraculous reveals God's character—His compassion, love, and desire to bring healing and restoration to His creation. Jesus performed miracles to show people the heart of the Father, demonstrating that God is not distant but deeply involved in our lives, ready to step in and bring about transformation.

The New Testament makes clear that these miracles are not limited to the past. As sons and daughters of God, filled with the Holy Spirit, we are called to operate in the miraculous. This is not an extraordinary calling reserved for a few special individuals; it is part of the normal Christian life.

The Holy Spirit empowers us to heal the sick, cast out demons, pray for miraculous provision, and more. The same power that raised Jesus from the dead lives in us; through that power, we are called to bring God's Kingdom into every area of life. Whether we are praying for a person to be healed of cancer or standing in faith for supernatural breakthrough in a crisis, the miraculous is a vital part of how God works through us to reveal His glory and advance His Kingdom.

Combining the Small and the Miraculous

The power of the small and the power of the miraculous are not opposing forces but complementary aspects of God's Kingdom. As sons and daughters of Christ's Ekkelesia, we are invited to operate in both realms, understanding that the Kingdom of God advances through subtle, everyday actions and supernatural interventions. The Holy Spirit equips us to do both.

Jesus Himself modeled this beautifully. From His relationship as Son with His Heavenly Father, Jesus performed miracles, healed the sick, and raised the dead, demonstrating God's miraculous power. Yet, He also spent time with people in small, intimate settings, sharing meals, teaching, and engaging in the everyday realities of life. He showed us that both the small and the miraculous are necessary for revealing the Father's love and bringing about transformation.

The power of the small works quietly and steadily, influencing culture and relationships over time. Like salt preserving food or light illuminating darkness, small acts of kindness, integrity, and sharing our testimony can have a profound and lasting impact. These daily acts may seem insignificant but done in the name of Jesus and in the power of the Holy Spirit, they set the stage for extraordinary transformation, often creating an environment where the supernatural can flourish.

At the same time, we are called to believe for and expect the miraculous. Miracles reveal the supernatural power of God and invite people into an encounter with His presence. They demonstrate that natural laws do not limit God and that His Kingdom operates on a higher level. When we pray for the sick and they are healed or see a miraculous breakthrough in times of need, we witness the Kingdom of God breaking into our world in tangible, powerful ways.

As sons and daughters of Christ's Ekklesia, we are empowered by the Holy Spirit to operate in the small and the miraculous. The same Spirit that equips us to be salt, light, and leaven in the world also empowers us to perform signs, wonders, and miracles. There is no division between the two—both are vital expressions of God's love and Kingdom, and keys that our Father has given us to fulfill His mission on Earth.

The small and the miraculous go hand in hand. They serve as keys to the Kingdom as we move through the Gates of Hades. As we engage in the small, faithful actions God calls us to, we create space for the miraculous to manifest. Likewise, witnessing the miraculous often allows us to continue influencing the world in the small, everyday moments that bring lasting change. God uses both to advance His Kingdom, and He has equipped us with everything we need through the power of the Holy Spirit.

Our role is to live from God, walking in the Spirit, whether through being salt and light in our daily interactions or believing in the miraculous when we pray for healing or provision. The Holy Spirit empowers us to do both, and as we apply these Kingdom keys, we reveal the fullness of God's love, power, and glory to a world in desperate need. We carry the Kingdom of God through everyday faithfulness, bringing transformation wherever we go. Both the small and the miraculous are essential tools in advancing God's Kingdom, and together, they enable us to fulfill our calling, rooted in our awakened identity, bringing His Kingdom to Earth as it is in Heaven. This is the normal Christian life.

10.
The World Awaits

In 2018, my wife, Wendi, and I traveled to the Philippines to minister to pastors and leaders through a series of three-day Ekklesia seminars across the nation. Our mission was to equip pastors and leaders to rise as Christ's governing body on Earth, but what unfolded during that time transformed us just as deeply as it did the pastors and leaders we ministered to. We arrived ready to share the Ekklesia teaching, yet what we encountered went far beyond anything we had imagined. The pastors we met were hungry for the revelation of Ekklesia, but we soon realized that many were already walking in the early revelation of their Sonship—laying a foundation that would allow them to embrace the fullness of their Kingdom identity.

At the same time, Wendi and I carried the message of Ekklesia, but our understanding of our full identity was still incomplete—we hadn't yet received the revelation of Sonship. We, too, were only partially awakened. Little did we know that God was preparing to awaken both sides of our identity—Sonship and Ekklesia—and something remarkable was about to happen in all of us.

As we began ministering, the Holy Spirit moved powerfully. These pastors already knew they were loved and adopted into

God's family as sons and daughters, but they hadn't yet grasped how their identity as sons and daughters gave them authority to function as Christ's Ekklesia. They had the love of the Father, but they lacked the full understanding of how that love empowered them to bring Heaven to Earth.

As this revelation settled into their hearts, an awakening took place. It wasn't just an emotional moment but a complete paradigm shift. These pastors began to see their calling differently. Their role wasn't confined to leading services or managing programs within church walls; they were called to transform their cities, communities, and nation. The realization that their identity as sons and daughters was inseparable from their function as Ekklesia revolutionized how they saw themselves and led their congregations.

What we witnessed was the start of a movement. Thousands of pastors embraced this revelation and took it back to their churches. We heard countless stories of God moving powerfully—burnt-out pastors being healed, marriages being restored, and churches awakening to their true purpose. The Holy Spirit was sparking something far more significant than personal transformation; it was a cultural reformation. The convergence of Sonship and Ekklesia spread like wildfire, igniting hearts and minds all over the country.

Recently, I spoke with the leaders who had first invited us to the Philippines, and their stories continue to inspire awe. Churches in the Philippines are no longer focused solely on what happens within their four walls; they actively engage their communities, bringing the Kingdom of God into every sphere of society—from education to business, from government to the arts. What began as individual transformation has become a national awakening.

This experience was also the beginning of an awakening for Wendi and me. Attending the weeklong A and B Schools, led by Father Heart Ministries from New Zealand, proved to be a pivotal experience. Interestingly, it was during our time in the Philippines that we first heard about these schools and encountered the deep revelation of the Father they carried. Witnessing Sonship being lived out so powerfully among the pastors and leaders there ignited something within us, propelling us into a transformational journey that reshaped our identity in the Father's love.

In the years that followed, the Holy Spirit continued to open our eyes to the fullness of His love and embrace. Just as they received their awakened identity, so did we—each of us growing into the fullness of what the Father had always intended.

We saw this firsthand in the Philippines. What begins as an internal shift within individuals has the power to grow, impacting entire communities and even reshaping a nation. As the Holy Spirit awakens people to their true identity, the ripple effect extends beyond their own lives—transforming families, influencing cities, and reaching nations with lasting impact. The transformation isn't contained—it expands naturally, carrying the power of the Kingdom into all areas of life.

Life in the Power of the Spirit

This brings us to a more profound question: How do we move beyond personal awakening to living out this awakened identity in the world around us? What happens when we live fully empowered by the Holy Spirit? This shift from individual transformation to a widespread move of God is where true awakening occurs—not just within us but in the families, communities, and nations we influence. The Holy Spirit invites us into a life where our awakened identity becomes a catalyst for revival, calling us to step into His power, not just for our sake but for the sake of the world.

Living from an awakened identity means living a life fully empowered by the Holy Spirit. This empowerment isn't reserved for a select few—it is available to every believer. Galatians 5:25 (NLT) reminds us, "Since we are living by the Spirit, let us follow the Spirit's leading in every part of our lives." This verse beautifully captures the essence of walking in your awakened identity, trusting the Holy Spirit to guide, strengthen, and equip you for all God has called you to.

It starts with the fruit of the Spirit—love, joy, peace, patience, kindness, goodness, faithfulness, gentleness, and self-control—becoming increasingly evident in our lives. We don't achieve these qualities through human effort; they are the supernatural result of a life surrendered to the Holy Spirit. As we walk in step with Him, His character is formed within us, transforming us from the inside out. This inner transformation lays the foundation for the Spirit's power to flow through us, where the culture within us begins to influence the culture around us.

Beyond this, the Holy Spirit also offers us the fullness of His power through baptism in the Holy Spirit. This power equips us to move in the gifts of the Spirit—to heal the sick, prophesy, perform miracles, and release the prophetic wherever we go. It's not about doing extraordinary things for personal platforms but about being vessels through which God's presence and power can flow, releasing His Kingdom on Earth.

Living by the Spirit is not just about personal transformation—it's about being empowered to bring Heaven to Earth. From an awakened identity, we are sent out with the Holy Spirit's wisdom, strength, and supernatural power to influence and transform the world around us. Whether in our families, workplaces, or communities, we carry the very presence of God. When we walk in step with the Spirit, every moment becomes an opportunity for God to move. Rather than a one-time experience, this is a continuous, dynamic partnership with the Holy Spirit that turns everyday life into a supernatural adventure.

Convictions That Change the World

There will be times when living out our awakened identity requires us to stand on convictions that bring us into confrontation with the world around us. Transformation doesn't avoid confrontation; it often demands it. In these moments, when our faith and identity collide with the world's values, distinctions are made, and God's glory is revealed. In the face of opposition, revival can spark, and nations can be changed. Knowing who we are gives us the strength to know what to do, even when the cost is high.

The story of Shadrach, Meshach, and Abednego in Daniel 3 is a powerful example of what it means to stand firm in your faith when everything around you is pressuring you to conform. These three men faced an impossible choice: bow down to the golden image that King Nebuchadnezzar had set up or face the fiery furnace. The king clarified his expectations: *"Now if you are ready to fall down and worship the image, all will be well. But if you do not, you will be thrown into the furnace"* (Daniel 3:15).

In the face of this ultimatum, Shadrach, Meshach, and Abednego made one of the boldest declarations of faith in Scripture: Daniel 3:18 (NIV) *"Even if God does not save us, we will not bow down to the statue."* This is the essence of *Even if* faith—an awakened faith from an awakened identity that refuses to compromise, even when the stakes are high. Their convictions were not based on whether God would deliver them from the fire; but their convictions were revealed in the fire. They knew who they were, and that knowledge anchored them in truth.

In the same way, we are called to live with unwavering convictions in a world that constantly pressures us to bow down to its idols—whether those idols are success, identity politics, or the approval of others. The world asks us to compromise our faith in exchange for comfort, status, or acceptance. But when we live from our awakened identity, we understand that our allegiance is to God alone. External pressures do not sway us because we know who we are and whom we serve.

Shadrach, Meshach, and Abednego's story didn't end with their declaration of faith. After they were thrown into the furnace, something miraculous happened: they were not alone. Nebuchadnezzar looked into the fire and saw a fourth man walking with them, who looked like "the Son of God" (Daniel 3:25). God didn't save them from the fire; He revealed Himself in it. This is our promise as well. When we stand firm in our convictions, God is with us in every trial, every fire, and every challenge.

And here's the most incredible part: after Shadrach, Meshach, and Abednego came out of the furnace unharmed, they were promoted. Nebuchadnezzar declared that their God was the true God and elevated them to positions of greater influence. This is what happens when we live with unwavering convictions from our awakened identity. Not only does God protect and sustain us, but He also promotes us. Our faith becomes a testimony that impacts kings, and God uses our convictions to bring about revival in the world.

There is no greater example than Jesus Himself. His identity as the Son of God led Him to the Cross, yet He did not waver. Fully aware of His mission to fulfill the will of the Father, Jesus pressed forward with unshakable conviction, even as He faced the agony of the Cross. His obedience wasn't driven by a desire to avoid suffering but by His unwavering commitment to fulfill His Father's purpose.

Just as Shadrach, Meshach, and Abednego declared *Even if*, so did Jesus. *Even if* the path led to the Cross, He chose to obey. His obedience to His Father brought about the greatest victory in history—salvation for all mankind. Through His sacrifice, Jesus was exalted and became the source of eternal life for all who believe. His life shows us that an unwavering conviction, rooted in our awakened identity, leads to personal victory and the transformation of the world.

As followers of Jesus, we are called to live with the same unwavering conviction. When we fully embrace our awakened identity, we realize our lives are woven into a greater purpose. Like Jesus, as sons and daughters of the Father, we are called to stand firm in the face of challenges, trusting that His purposes will always prevail.

As sons and daughters of God, we stay connected to His love, and as His Ekklesia, we bring His Kingdom into every place we go. Hold fast to all God has placed on your heart and refuse to waver in the face of opposition. When challenges arise, stand firm in who you are and the calling you carry.

Where to Begin

Now that you've been awakened to your identity as a son or daughter and empowered by the Holy Spirit as Christ's Ekklesia, you may ask, "Where do I begin?" How do you practically live out this awakened identity and start bringing Heaven to Earth? Here are twelve essential steps that will help guide you as you take your first steps into this new life of purpose and power.

1. *Cultivate Intimacy with Your Father*
   Everything begins with your relationship with God. This isn't just about religious rituals or checking off a prayer list—it's about a deep connection with your Heavenly Father. Set aside a dedicated time each day to spend with Him. Use that time to grow closer to God in prayer, worship, or reading the Bible. Don't rush through it. Ask Him to speak to you and be still enough to listen. Take moments to lean into His presence and hear His voice. As you deepen your intimacy with the Father, you will find that everything you do flows naturally from that connection.

2. *Learn how to be led by the Holy Spirit*
   The Holy Spirit has been given to you as a Guide, Counselor, and Teacher. To live from your awakened identity, you must learn how to be led by Him daily. Start each day by asking the Holy Spirit to guide you. As you go about your day, be aware of His promptings, whether in decisions, conversations, or opportunities. The more you listen and respond, the more sensitive you'll become to His voice. Don't be afraid to step out in faith when you feel the Holy Spirit leading you to encourage someone, pray for someone, or act in a way that seems unexpected. The more you trust Him, the more you'll see His power at work in and through you.

3. *Live from God, not for God*
   Living from God, not for God, means shifting from striving to please Him through our efforts to embracing a life that flows out of His love and grace. Instead of constantly trying to earn approval or achieve spiritual milestones, we rest in our identity as His children, living from the overflow, as we allow His Spirit to work through us. This looks like starting

each day by asking the Father to fill us with His love (Romans 5:5) and choosing to depend on the Holy Spirit, trusting Him to guide our decisions, empower our actions, and shape our character. It's about letting go of the pressure to perform and learning to walk in step with His leading, where our lives become an overflow of His presence. In reality, when you prioritize living from God, you will find yourself living for God.

4. *Declare and Prophesy Over Your Future*
   Your words carry the power of life and death, and as a child of God, you have been given the authority to declare His promises over your life. Begin by speaking God's truth over yourself and your circumstances. Say out loud the things God has promised you in His Word, like "I am more than a conqueror (Romans 8:37)" or His plans "to give you a hope and a future" (Jeremiah 29:11 NIV)." As you grow in this, ask your Heavenly Father to give you prophetic insight into your future. When you sense Him leading you in a specific direction, speak it out with faith. Prophesy over your life, believing that the Father is guiding your steps and preparing a future filled with His plans and purposes.

5. *Live with a Kingdom Mindset*
   Living with a Kingdom mindset means viewing everything in life through the lens of God's Kingdom. Your work, relationships, and even how you respond to challenges should be shaped by the knowledge that you represent God's Kingdom on Earth. Matthew 6:33 says to seek the Kingdom of God and His righteousness first and all these things shall be added to you. Let this truth shape your decisions and priorities. Pray regularly for God's Kingdom to come in your family,

work, and city, knowing that you are part of His plan to bring Heaven to Earth.

6. *Step Out in Signs, Wonders, and Miracles*
The Holy Spirit has empowered you to walk in the supernatural. This means that signs, wonders, and miracles should be part of your everyday life. When someone expresses a need or a challenge, take the bold step of offering to pray for them as the Holy Spirit leads you. Don't wait for the perfect moment—pray on the spot and believe that God will move. Expect miracles, not just in church but in your workplace, at home, and in your community. Study the Bible's accounts of healing and miracles and let them build your faith. As you see the Lord move through your prayers and acts of faith, keep track of what He's doing so you can testify and encourage others to step out in bold faith.

7. *Look for Ways to Serve Others*
Jesus modeled servant leadership, and we are called to serve as His followers. Look around you and ask God to open your eyes to the needs of those in your church, family, and community. Whether helping someone practically, lending a listening ear, or offering prayer, be willing to serve without expecting anything in return. Jesus had the anointing without measure and was the servant of all. Serving others is one of the most powerful ways to demonstrate the love of Christ and grow in the anointing. Seek out ways to serve others regularly, and you will find that God uses your service to bring His Kingdom to Earth.

8. *Find and Use the Gifts the Father Has Given You*
   The Father has placed unique gifts and talents inside you for a specific purpose. These are not just for your personal fulfillment but for expanding His Kingdom. Take time to discover those gifts by seeking the Lord in prayer and asking the Holy Spirit to reveal how He wants you to use them. Your gifts—whether teaching, hospitality, leadership, creativity, or something else—are vital to the body of Christ. Don't allow your gifts to remain dormant; instead, *stir up* the gifts inside you (2 Timothy 1:6). Step out in faith, develop your abilities, and trust that the Lord will open doors of opportunity for you to use them to glorify Him and serve others. The more you walk in your gifting, the more you will see how the Father has designed you to impact the world.

9. *Find Your Tribe*
   You are not meant to live out your faith alone. God created us for community, and finding a group of people—your tribe—walking in their awakened identity is essential. Surround yourself with others who will encourage, challenge, and help you grow. Just as iron sharpens iron, these relationships will refine you and keep you grounded in your pursuit of God's Kingdom. A crucial part of finding your tribe is committing to your local church. The church (Ekklesia) is where you will build deep, lasting relationships, serve together, and be part of something larger than yourself. By investing in your local church community, you will find friends and a spiritual family who will walk with you as you live out your calling. Your faith will be strengthened as you serve alongside others, and you will help strengthen theirs.

10. *Be Salt, Light, and Leaven in the Workplace*
    Your workplace is more than a place to earn a paycheck—it's your mission field. Jesus called us to be the salt of the Earth, the light of the world, and the leaven that transforms from within. In your workplace, you are called to reflect Christ. This means modeling integrity, kindness, and excellence in everything you do. Look for opportunities to pray for your coworkers or encourage them when they're going through tough times. Ask the Holy Spirit to use you to transform your workplace by living out biblical values and influencing those around you with Christ's love. Every day is an opportunity to be a witness to the goodness of God.

11. *Engage the Spheres in Your City*
    You are not placed in your city by accident—the Lord has positioned you there with purpose. He calls you to be an agent of transformation, influencing every part of society with His Kingdom. The key spheres that shape culture—family, government, business, education, media, arts and entertainment, and the church—hold significant power in forming values, beliefs, and behaviors. Whether you are actively working in one of these spheres or feel called to impact another, your presence can bring change.

    Transformation begins with prayer. Intercede for your city's leaders, schools, and neighborhoods, asking your Heavenly Father to bring revival and healing. But prayer alone isn't enough—take action. Get involved in local initiatives that align with biblical values, whether through volunteering, engaging in community events, or stepping into leadership roles. If the Lord is stirring your heart for greater influence, consider participating in local government or other decision-making spaces to be a voice for righteousness and justice. Your city is part of God's plan, and He has placed you there to make a difference.

12. *Share the Gospel*
Your most important mission is to share the good news of Jesus Christ with others. You have been called to be a witness of His love, salvation, and grace. Start by sharing your testimony—how God has worked in your life and transformed you. Don't be afraid to discuss your faith with friends, family, and coworkers. When the opportunity arises, offer to pray for people and share the hope found in Jesus. Whether through personal conversations or supporting outreach ministries, your mission is to bring the gospel's message to a world that desperately needs it.

These twelve starting points aren't just practices, they're pathways to a life fully awakened in identity and purpose. As you walk them out, you won't just see change in your life—you become the change your friends, family, workplace and the world have been waiting for. The time isn't someday. The time is now.

You don't need to have it all figured out. Just begin. Take one step, then another, and trust that as you move forward, God will lead you with grace, wisdom and power. The world doesn't need perfection, it needs sons and daughters who are awake and willing.

That's what the next chapter is all about, to rise, take your place, and walk in the fullness of your awakened identity.

11.
This is Your Time

Romans 8:19 declares, "For the earnest expectation of the creation eagerly waits for the revealing of the sons of God." While this passage points to a future glory, I believe its truth is just as relevant today. The world is yearning, longing for something it can't fully comprehend but desperately needs. And it's waiting for you. Creation itself is groaning for the sons and daughters of God to rise, step into their God-given authority, and move out as Christ's Ekklesia, in their awakened identity, manifesting the Kingdom of Heaven here on Earth. The time has come for you to take your place in God's glorious plan, ignite revival, and be part of the global awakening the world is aching for. Now is the moment for you to walk in the fullness of your identity and unleash the transformative power of the Kingdom.

You've moved past the orphan state that once held you captive. No longer bound by fear, striving, or living under the weight of dos and don'ts, you've embraced your true identity as a son or daughter of God. You are no longer defined by the limitations of the law or the mindset of an orphan but by the freedom that comes from knowing you are fully accepted, fully loved, and fully empowered by the Father. You've entered into the fullness of Sonship, and now, from this place of victory, you are walking in the

Spirit, led by His voice, empowered by His presence, and carrying the authority you were always meant to have.

This is your time—a summons to step boldly into your awakened identity and bring the Kingdom of God into the world around you. Your family, community, workplace, and nation are longing to step into the fullness of the Father's design for them, yet they cannot do it alone. You are positioned to carry the message of the Kingdom into these spaces, awakening those around you to the life the Father has destined for them.

The people God has placed in your life and the world He has connected you to are ready to experience the fullness of your awakened identity as it is fully revealed in Christ and lived out through you. They need what you carry, and now is the moment to step confidently into your calling, bringing the Kingdom of Heaven into every sphere you touch.

Paul spoke of the "revealing" of the sons of God, and now, that revelation is unfolding in your life. As you live out your awakened identity, walking with boldness, faith, and unwavering conviction, the world begins to take notice. Your authority is no longer hidden. Your faith, courage, and willingness to stand firm in the face of challenges are a testament to the transformative power of the Father's work within you. The world will witness His Kingdom advancing through your life. You have awakened—and now, creation itself rejoices as you take your place in God's divine plan to bring Heaven to Earth.

Step Into What's Possible

In *Hacksaw Ridge*, Desmond Doss's story illustrates a powerful awakening to his identity and purpose. As he puts on his uniform, he steps into a role not as a typical soldier but as one called to save lives rather than take them. Facing intense ridicule and immense pressure, he holds firmly to his conviction to serve without carrying a weapon. Yet, on the battlefield, under the most harrowing conditions, Desmond discovers what is possible. His commitment to his faith and calling awakens a strength he never knew he possessed, empowering him to rescue dozens of his fellow soldiers. With each life he saves, he prays, "Lord, help me get one more." Driven by this unshakable purpose, he keeps returning to the battlefield, one rescue at a time, revealing what is possible when we fully become who we are called to be.

Desmond's story vividly portrays what stepping into an awakened identity means—a calling that transforms him into a vessel of courage, compassion, and strength. His story reveals how, when we lean into our God-given identity, we are empowered to do the impossible and bring hope and transformation, even in the most desperate places. Desmond's life reminds us that, with God's strength, our awakened identity can save lives.

You are chosen by the Father, adopted into His family through the finished work of Jesus, and filled with His Spirit. Wherever you go, the presence of God goes with you. You are not ordinary—you are a son or daughter of your Heavenly Father, and you carry the authority of Heaven. Every place you step and every word you speak carries the potential to release Heaven, impacting lives and shaping culture. The question is not whether you have been called but whether you will step into that calling. This is your time—to walk in the fullness of your awakened identity and bring the Kingdom of God wherever you go.

Too often, we fall into the trap of believing the lie that we're not ready or qualified. We convince ourselves that someone else is more capable, spiritual, or equipped. But the truth is, God doesn't wait for us to be qualified—He qualifies those He calls. He has already called you and given you everything you need. The same Spirit that raised Jesus from the dead lives in you. You are equipped, you are empowered, and you are enough. The enemy aims to keep you sidelined, doubting your worth and questioning your call. But now is the time to reject those lies, step into the fullness of your identity, and rise up.

Look at the disciples—ordinary men with no special qualifications. Yet, after encountering the risen Christ and being filled with the Holy Spirit, they changed the world. Like Desmond saving lives on the battlefield, these disciples stepped onto a spiritual battlefield, praying, *"Lord, help us get one more."* By living from their awakened identity, they witnessed whole cities transformed. Though they were not impressive in the world's eyes, they were sons and daughters of their Heavenly Father, who legislated as Christ's Ekklesia in the power of the Holy Spirit, making them unstoppable. Embracing their awakened identity, they went out boldly, performing miracles, healing the sick, and turning cities upside down for God's glory. Desmond's story echoes what we saw in the disciples—as they realized who they were and stepped out in faith, trusting God to work through them. This is what is possible when we fully embrace our awakened identity.

Called to More

For so many, Christianity has settled into a series of well-meaning but predictable routines. People go to church on Sunday, maybe midweek too, pray and read a few verses each morning, and check the boxes of good Christian behavior. These are all good things, but is this really the fullness of what it means to be a son or daughter of God? Are we meant to live our lives according to a checklist, or is there a more profound calling, a greater purpose, that reaches beyond our comfort zones?

What if you were called to be more than a church attender? What if you were called to be a world changer? Imagine stepping into an awakened identity where you are not just practicing faith but carrying the Father's love and presence into every part of your world. What if your life, rooted in Sonship, could impact the world in drawing people into the love of Christ?

This is the invitation—to enter into a life of purpose, power, and true transformation. You're called not just to participate but to partner with Heaven, to bring the Kingdom of God wherever you go. So, don't settle for the mundane but rather, rise as part of the Ekklesia, walking boldly in the fullness of your awakened identity.

You are called to live as a vessel of God's presence and power. You carry the Kingdom of God within you, and it is not for your benefit alone—it is for the world around you. When you live from your awakened identity, you will walk differently, love courageously, and speak with authority. You will see opportunities for breakthrough where others see barriers. You will bring hope where there is despair. You will reflect Christ in all that you do.

Living from your awakened identity is not about playing it safe. It's about partnering with God for revival and reformation. This is not about your own strength or wisdom; it's about yielding to the Holy Spirit and trusting Him to guide you. It's about stepping out in faith, even when you don't have all the answers, and believing that God will meet you in every step.

The Father has positioned you for *such a time as this*. There will be moments of uncertainty when fear presses in, but those are the moments to remind yourself of who you are in Christ. You are a son. You are a daughter. You are loved, chosen, empowered, and sent. God is with you, and He will never leave you.

Like Mordecai and Esther, your identity and calling are woven into God's divine plan. Mordecai stood unwavering in his convictions, refusing to bow to Haman, demonstrating our functional identity as Ekklesia—a bold stand that acts, confronts evil, and legislates righteousness. Esther, on the other hand, operated in her relational identity. She didn't win the king's heart through initially confronting evil or legislating righteousness, but through intimacy, connecting with his heart through love and grace. Together, their distinct identities worked harmoniously, leading to a divine reversal that saved a nation in a single day. And just like Esther, who was positioned *for such a time as this*, you, too, have been placed in this moment to step into your relational and functional identity, bringing God's Kingdom to Earth in the time and place He has called you to.

We, too, have the potential for such divine impact. The world around us—our families, communities, and nations—are in desperate need of Jesus, not only as Lord and Savior but as the One who brings them out of their orphaned existence and into the loving embrace of the Father. When we live from our awakened identity as sons and daughters of the King, we step into the authority and intimacy that bring transformation. Just as a nation was saved through the boldness and grace of Mordecai and Esther, we are called to stand in our awakened identity and partner with Him to do the same.

Imagine a world where every believer came into the fullness of their awakened identity, embracing their authority, walking in the power of the Spirit, and bringing the Kingdom of God into their everyday lives. Churches would be renewed, cities would be impacted, nations would be changed, and revival would break out in places once considered hopeless. This is not a far-off fantasy—it's the reality the Father is inviting you into. You are part of His plan to bring Heaven to Earth.

Will you step into the fullness of who God has created you to be? Will you silence the doubts, the fears, and the excuses and say yes to the position and calling God has placed on your life? When we do our lives become more than a personal journey, they become a source of something the world desperately needs: hope.

Carriers of Hope

As sons and daughters walking in our awakened identity, we are not only transformed by the love of God—we become carriers of hope. This hope, ignited within our hearts by the revelation of who we are in the Father's love, empowers us to live differently. It is the unshakable confidence that God is with us, that His promises are true, and that we are part of His divine plan for the world. This hope radiates from within, shaping our thoughts, decisions, and actions, and anchoring us in the truth of God's goodness.

As carriers of hope, we present it to the world around us. We step into places others avoid—we *encourage* those who are struggling, *lift* the spirits of friends caught in despair, and *stand* beside people battling addiction or loss. We bring hope by speaking truth where lies have taken root, showing kindness where bitterness has built walls, and shining light into the darkest places. Hope flows from us, inviting others to see that there is a God who knows them, loves them, and can transform their lives.

Our lives align with the Father's purpose, reflecting His heart and Kingdom. In every interaction in every environment, we bring the possibility of restoration and redemption. As we walk in our awakened identity, we light up the darkness with hope, offering the world words and living examples of an authentic, Christ-centered life. This is our calling—to carry the hope that comes from Jesus into every corner of the world, sharing the love and truth of the gospel with a world desperately in need of Him.

Partner with Heaven

As you reach these final pages, the call to walk in your awakened identity extends far beyond these chapters. Your awakened identity is a call to partner with Heaven, to live with purpose and intentionality. You are called not only to experience this truth but to walk it out daily, influencing the world around you for the glory of God. This isn't a one-time realization; it's a lifelong adventure of partnering with your Father for personal and cultural transformation.

Think of Simba in *The Lion King*. When he looks into the water, he finally sees his true reflection—he sees his father in himself, a powerful reminder of who he really is. At that moment, Simba hears his father's voice: "Remember who you are." The revelation of his identity awakens him to his destiny, urging him to rise and fulfill his calling. Like Simba, once you've awakened to your true identity, it's time to do something with it. You're called to step into your purpose and bring hope and restoration to the world around you.

It doesn't matter how ordinary you feel or how flawed your past may be. God has chosen you, equipped you, and filled you with His power. When you walk in your awakened identity, you carry a light that pierces the darkness, a love that heals wounds, and a strength that lifts those who are weary. Your life can break chains, heal broken hearts, and inspire others to seek the God who transformed you.

So, how can you change your world? It begins by being filled daily with the love of the Father, and humbly showing up in the fullness of who God has made you to be. With each small act of faith, word of encouragement, and bold stand for truth, you become the change the world desperately needs. Embrace your identity, yield to the Holy Spirit, and watch how the Father partners with you to bring hope, healing, and transformation to a world waiting for someone to show them the way.

Awaken Others

You can also fulfill your awakened identity by sharing this message. Pass along this book to someone who needs to discover the depth of who they are meant to be in Christ. Let the truth of Sonship and Ekklesia empower others to step into the fullness of their identity in Christ.

Pass along this message of Sonship to others. Think of the countless people around you—friends, family members, coworkers—who may still be searching, striving, and questioning their worth, unaware of their incredible inheritance in Christ. Imagine the impact you can have by helping them discover who they truly are as sons and daughters of God. Pass along this book to someone who needs to see themselves through the eyes of their Heavenly Father, who needs to experience the freedom and purpose found in an awakened identity in Christ.

Let the truth of Sonship and Ekklesia empower others to step boldly into their calling. As you share this message, you're not just giving them words—you're offering a lifeline, an invitation to step out of the shadows of insecurity and into a life of purpose, love, and Kingdom expansion. And with each conversation and act of sharing, you, too, will find your understanding of Sonship deepening. There is something profound about seeing others awaken that also strengthens and solidifies the revelation within us. Walking this path together, we gain new layers of insight, confidence, and strength.

Together, we're part of something greater than ourselves. We are a family, called to be Christ's Ekklesia, His legislative assembly, on Earth. By passing this message forward, you're inviting others into the fullness of their identity in Christ. This is your opportunity to empower others to rise, stand, and walk in the authority they've been given. Imagine the world that could unfold as each one of us steps into the fullness of our identity and encourages others to do the same. Be a catalyst of this awakening, allowing it to transform you and change those around you.

Awakened Together to Change the World

As you step into your awakened identity, I invite you to join a global community of believers committed to living out this truth. At WorldChangerHQ, we bring together those who are being awakened to their identity in Sonship and Ekklesia, equipping and empowering them to influence every sphere of society for God's glory. You don't have to walk this journey alone. In community, we grow together, strengthening our identity, deepening our impact, and bringing personal renewal that leads to cultural transformation. As we stand alongside one another, we gain the confidence to walk fully in who we are called to be and the courage to live it out.

If you are ready to take the next step, to go deeper in your awakened identity and connect with like-minded believers passionate about living from God's presence and advancing His Kingdom, visit worldchangerhq.com. You'll find encouragement and strength as you grow in your awakened identity through live-stream events, hands-on workshops, weekly challenges, and vibrant community engagement.

This community is a place to experience life-giving connections with others walking in their awakened identity—growing together in Sonship and Ekklesia, strengthening one another in faith, and stepping into the fullness of who we are called to be. But it doesn't stop there. As a legislative assembly, we are not just called to be transformed ourselves but to advance God's purposes in the world—bringing revival, discipling nations, and seeing His Kingdom established in every sphere of society.

Imagine stepping into your calling with a family of believers who champion you, stand with you, and pursue God's purposes together. Here, you'll find encouragement, strength, and the courage to step boldly into the impact you were created to make.

Lastly, I want you to know, I'm on this journey too. God is still awakening things in me. I'm continually learning what it means to live as a son and to let that identity shape everything I do. And when it comes to the Ekklesia, I'm still breaking free of old church-paradigm mindsets and stepping deeper into the mission Jesus gave us, to advance His Kingdom beyond the walls of the church. I often find myself asking the Father for wisdom, so I can fully partner with what Jesus is building-and lead others into it. An awakened identity isn't the finish line-it's the beginning of a spirit-led life.

You are now part of a growing company of sons and daughters, awakened to their identity and ready to live as Christ's Ekklesia. As world changers, we influence culture and bring the Kingdom wherever we go. From an awakened identity, let's change the world, one life at a time, for God's glory.

Scan the QR code to connect with a growing network of believers living out their Awakened Identity to change the world through WorldChangerHQ.

About the Author

Greg Simas is the founder and senior pastor of Convergence Church in the San Francisco Bay Area, where he has led with passion and vision for over 30 years. He is also the founder and leader of Convergence School of Ministry, equipping and deploying people to bring personal and cultural transformation. Greg is deeply committed to helping believers live from their identity as sons and daughters of the Father while bringing transformation beyond the walls of the church. Through his leadership, preaching, and coaching, he has equipped countless believers to walk in their God-given authority and embrace their role as Christ's *Ekklesia*, advancing His kingdom into every sphere of society.

    A sought-after speaker, mentor, and teacher, Greg is passionate about revival, biblical identity, and empowering the body of Christ to walk in supernatural power. His ministry is marked by both spiritual depth and practical action, equipping believers to integrate their faith into every area of life. He and his wife, Wendi, have been married for 40 years and are blessed with a growing family, including their children and grandchildren. Whether through his writing, coaching, or ministry, he remains committed to seeing lives transformed as they embrace their awakened identity, walk in their God-given authority, and advance His Kingdom on Earth as it is in Heaven.

Convergence Church

Discover Convergence Church—a community of believers devoted to God's presence, rooted in biblical truth, and passionate about transforming culture. Together, we are embracing and living out an awakened identity in every sphere of life, bringing heaven to earth. Scan the QR code to access sermons, resources, and opportunities to pursue revival with us.

https://www.ccfremont.org/

Convergence School of Ministry

Discover how you can be equipped and released into your identity and calling through Convergence School of Ministry. Our passion is to awaken and empower believers in their sonship and as Christ's Ekklesia, carrying the Father's heart and advancing His Kingdom in every sphere of life. Scan the QR code to learn more about courses, training, and how you can be a part of this movement.

https://www.convergence.school/

www.ingramcontent.com/pod-product-compliance
Lightning Source LLC
Chambersburg PA
CBHW070330010526
44107CB00004B/481